TWENTY-FIRST CENTURY TEACHING GUIDE FOR INDIAN SCHOOLS

SOCIAL SCIENCE BOOK I

Suvraleena Bandyopadhyay is based in Kolkata and is a seasoned teacher and examiner with expertise across international and Indian education boards. She brings the past alive with her dynamic teaching style showing students how the social sciences shape the world we live in today. With years of classroom and assessment experience, Suvraleena continues to be fascinated by the stories History tells, the terrains Geography uncovers, the power of Civics and by the infinite opportunities that the social sciences hold to inspire the future.

PEDAGOGY SERIES

Twenty-First Century

TEACHING GUIDE FOR INDIAN SCHOOLS

Social Science 1

Suvraleena Bandyopadhyay

For Classes
3–5

hachette INDIA

First published in 2025 by Hachette India
(Registered name: Hachette Book Publishing India Pvt. Ltd)
An Hachette UK company
www.hachetteindia.com

1

ISBN: 978-93-5731-457-2

Hachette Book Publishing India Pvt. Ltd
4th & 5th Floors, Corporate Centre
Plot No. 94, Sector 44, Gurugram – 122003, India

Typeset in Adobe Garamond Pro 11.5/16
by R. Ajith Kumar
New Delhi

MIX
Paper | Supporting responsible forestry
FSC® C010615

Printed and bound in India
by Thomson Press India Ltd.

Contents

Chapter 1

NEP, NCF and Twenty-first Century Skills

THE NATIONAL EDUCATION POLICY, 2020, observes education as fundamental for achieving full human potential, developing an equitable and just society and promoting national development. Access to universal quality education is the key to India's continued ascent and leadership on the global stage in terms of economic growth, social justice and equality, scientific advancement, national integration and cultural preservation. This is regarded as the best way forward for developing and maximizing our country's rich talents and resources for the good of the individual, the society, the country and the world. India will have the highest population of young people in the world over the next decade, and our ability to provide high-quality educational opportunities to all will determine the future of our country.[1]

After a careful study of the fundamental principles of NEP 2020, we find a lot of common ground between these principles and the twenty-first century skills. The fundamental principles of NEP 2020 are as follows:

- Recognizing, identifying, and fostering the unique capabilities of each student.
- According the highest priority to achieving foundational literacy and numeracy.
- Flexibility.
- No hard separations between arts and sciences, between curricular and extracurricular activities, between vocational and academic streams, etc.
- Multidisciplinary and holistic education.
- Emphasis on conceptual understanding.
- Creativity and critical thinking.
- Ethics and human and Constitutional values.
- Promoting multilingualism and the power of language.
- Life skills.
- Focus on regular formative assessment for learning.
- Extensive use of technology.
- Respect for diversity and respect for the local context.
- Full equity and inclusion.
- Synergy in curriculum across all levels of education.
- Teachers and faculty as the heart of the learning process.
- A 'light but tight' regulatory framework to ensure integrity, transparency and resource efficiency.
- Outstanding research.

- Continuous review.
- A rootedness and pride in India.
- Education as a public service.
- Substantial investment in a strong, vibrant public education system.[2]

For the holistic development of learners, the NEP 2020 states that the key overall thrust of curriculum and pedagogy reform across all stages should be to move the education system towards real understanding and learning how to learn. This means, we need to take a step away from the culture of rote learning, which, unfortunately, is largely present today. The aim of education should not only be cognitive development but also building character and creating holistic and well-rounded individuals who are equipped with key Twenty-first century skills.

Knowledge is seen to be a deep-seated treasure, and education helps in its manifestation as the perfection that is already within an individual. All aspects of curriculum and pedagogy need to be reoriented to attain these critical goals. Specific sets of skills and values across domains will be identified for integration and incorporation at each stage of learning, from preschool to higher education.

Curriculum frameworks need to be developed to ensure that these skills and values are imbibed through engaging processes of teaching and learning. There needs to be a reduction in curriculum content to enhance essential learning and critical thinking. Curriculum content in each subject needs to have its core essentials to make space for critical thinking and more holistic, inquiry-based, discovery-based, discussion-based and analysis-based learning. The content will focus on key concepts, ideas, applications and problem-solving. Teaching and learning to be conducted in a more interactive manner. Questions are encouraged, and classroom sessions should regularly contain more fun, creative, collaborative and exploratory activities for students for deeper and more experiential learning.

In all stages, experiential learning, including hands-on learning, arts-integrated and sports-integrated education and storytelling-based pedagogy, among others, should become standard pedagogy. This form of learning is essential for explorations of relations among different subjects as well. To close the gap in the achievement of learning outcomes, classroom transactions need to shift towards competency-based learning and education.

Art integration is a cross-curricular pedagogical approach that aims to utilize various aspects and forms of art and culture as the basis for learning of concepts across subjects. As a part of the thrust on experiential learning, art-integrated education needs to be embedded in classroom transactions not only for creating joyful classrooms but also for imbibing the Indian ethos through integration of Indian art and culture in the teaching and learning process at every level. This art-integrated approach will strengthen the linkages between education and culture.

Sports integration is another cross-curricular pedagogical approach that employs physical activities, including indigenous sports, in pedagogical practices to help develop skills such as collaboration, self-initiative, self-direction, self-discipline, teamwork, responsibility, citizenship, etc. Sports-integrated learning, when undertaken in classrooms, helps students to adopt fitness as a lifelong attitude and to achieve the related life skills along with the levels of fitness as envisaged in the Fit India Movement. The need to integrate sports in education is well recognized as it serves to foster holistic development by promoting physical and psychological well-being while also enhancing cognitive abilities.

Empowering students through flexibility in course choices is another area that needs dedicated attention. Students will be given increased flexibility and choice of subjects to study, particularly in secondary school – including subjects in physical education, the arts and crafts and vocational skills – so that they can design their own paths of study and life plans. Holistic development and a wide choice of subjects and courses year to year are to be the new distinguishing features of school education. There will be no hard separation among 'curricular', 'extracurricular', or 'co-curricular', among 'arts', 'humanities' and 'sciences' or between 'vocational' or 'academic' streams. Subjects like physical education, arts and crafts and vocational skills, in addition to science, humanities, and mathematics, will be incorporated throughout the school curriculum with a consideration for what is interesting and safe at each age.

The NEP 2020 also aims to restructure school curriculum and pedagogy in a new 5+3+3+4 design. The curricular and pedagogical structure of school education will be reconfigured to make it more responsive and relevant to the developmental needs and interests of learners at different stages of their development, corresponding to the age ranges of 3–8, 8–11, 11–14, and 14–18 years, respectively. This structure will constitute the Foundational Stage (covering ages 3–8), Preparatory Stage (grades 3–5, covering ages 8–11), Middle Stage (grades 6–8, covering ages 11–14) and Secondary Stage (grades 9–12 in two phases, covering ages 14–18).[3]

Table 1: NEP, NCF and Twenty-first century Skills

Theme on focus	**NEP 2020**	**NCF**	**Twenty-first century skills**
Learner-centric approach (Personalized learning)	Recognizing and fostering unique capabilities	Supporting learner autonomy and promoting rational thinking	Focus on learner autonomy and adaptability
Integrated and Flexible approach	No hard separations between disciplines	Interdisciplinary participation (for example cultural, economic integration)	Cross disciplinary problem solving

Theme on focus	NEP 2020	NCF	Twenty-first century skills
Critical thinking	Emphasis on conceptual understanding, creativity & critical thinking	Focus on rational thought	Critical thinking, problem solving
Ethics	Ethics, human & Constitutional values	Democratic & community participation	Global citizenship, ethics
Life skills	Life skills, respect for diversity, inclusion	Health, well-being, community participation	Communication skills, cultural, media literacy
Use of technology	Integration of technology in teaching-learning processes	Use of technology as a support tool	Digital literacy, ICT skills
Inclusive Education	Equity and inclusion	Equal participation for all	Inclusivity, accessibility

In order to implement activities related to student assessment along with other tasks as mandated by the National Education Policy, 2020, PARAKH (Performance Assessment, Review and Analysis of Knowledge for Holistic Development) was set up in NCERT as an independent constituent unit. This unit is to also to fulfil the basic objectives of setting norms, standards and guidelines as stated by the NEP 2020.

PARAKH has designed the Holistic Progress Card (HPC) for the Preparatory Stage to help teachers and educators in India monitor the progress of their learners throughout the academic year. This holistic card acknowledges the multifaceted nature of learning at this stage, ensuring that young minds are not only equipped with foundational academic skills but are also nurtured emotionally and creatively.

Among other useful information and teaching aids, the HPC provides assistance to teachers with learning standards. For example, the learning standards for 'The World around Us' in the Preparatory Stage include:

Topic: Saving a River

Assumptions: Learners have already read a chapter about water pollution in their state and how an important river is slowly dying. They have answered comprehension questions and have done some activities to understand water pollution. In groups, they have been preparing a story on the same topic.

Learning Outcome: Learners will be able to present a skit about water pollution and how it can be prevented.

Activity Duration: 40 minutes

Activity Flow

Time	Probable steps
5 mins	Teacher leads a classroom discussion on how water pollution can be prevented and reminds children to include as many elements as possible.
10 mins	Learners do a demo of their skits/one-acts within their group. Teacher monitors and offers feedback/help.
20 mins	Learners present their skits, and peers offer feedback.
5 mins	Teacher does a feedback session and talks about steps that can be taken to save their local river/ water source.

The purpose of the National Curriculum Framework for School Education (NCF-SE, in short, NCF) is to help bring about the changes stated in the NEP 2020 by effecting corresponding positive transformations in India's school curricula.

In this NCF, 'curriculum' refers to the overall goals, plans, arrangements and practices that shape the experiences of learners in schools. Thus, 'curriculum' does not just refer to the subject content of textbooks and other teaching-learning materials (TLMs) and their pedagogy but also includes aspects like school environment and culture. It is indeed only through such holistic and integrated changes across all the key aspects of the curriculum that one will be able to positively transform the overall learning experiences of our students.

The Learning Standards given below are guided by certain widely agreed upon broad Aims of School Education that are articulated in the NCF. These aims have been arrived at from the vision and purpose of education as envisaged by NEP 2020:

a. **Rational Thought and Autonomy.** Schools should aim to develop independent thinkers who make well-informed decisions. These decisions are to be based on a grounded understanding of the world around us.
b. **Health and Well-being.** School education should be a wholesome experience for students. They should acquire knowledge, capacities, and dispositions that promote mind-body wellness.
c. **Democratic and Community Participation.** Democracy is not just a form of governance, it is a 'mode of associated living', a sense of collaborative community. School education should aim to develop such knowledge, capacities, and values and dispositions that enable learners to participate and contribute to the democratic functioning of the country.
d. **Economic Participation.** School education should aim to develop such knowledge, capacities, values, and dispositions that enable learners to participate and contribute to the economy. Effective participation in the

economy has a positive impact both on the individual and on society as a whole.

e. **Cultural Participation.** Understanding the culture and heritage embedded in the family and community is at the core of cultural participation. School education should aim to promote cultural literacy and enable students to acquire knowledge, capacities, and values and dispositions to participate meaningfully and contribute positively to culture.[4]

The purpose of social science education is multifaceted. It helps students to learn about the society in which they live – how members of their society live, interact, behave, eat, speak (and in what languages), express themselves through art, the traditions they follow, the clothes they wear and their aspirations. It also helps students to understand their origins, their ancestors, their culture, their neighbours, and consequently, themselves. Social science education introduces students to people whom they have never met, places that they have never been to, stories that they have never heard and new ideas that they have never conceived, thereby expanding their horizons and opening their minds to new possibilities. Finally, social science education helps students develop pride in their culture and their country, with a forward-looking spirit to continuously improve – as individuals, as a society and as a nation.[5]

Let us integrate some strategies for teaching social science mentioned in the NCF with some Twenty-first century skills-based concepts and terminologies. We will discuss the 21st century skills in further details in the upcoming chapters.

1. **NCF:** Inquiry-based methods help learners understand how social scientists generate knowledge. For example, learners can make and test hypotheses about factors that influence migration in their locality or region, the genesis of various settlement patterns in their region, why specific types of occupations are more prevalent in specific regions and so on.

   Project work: Effective social science teaching happens when students collaborate on a project or a specific task. These could be conducting surveys and interviews (e.g., household surveys, interviews with stakeholders of the society, such as the village sarpanch), drawing a map of their classroom, investigating historical sources in their region, tabulating the types of bazaars/markets. Such projects should be designed collaboratively along with students with sufficient time given to collect data, analyse it and present it in the classrooms.

   Some specific opportunities for projects to create models and artefacts: Students should be given opportunities where they can apply their knowledge to create models and artefacts. These could be in the form of poster-making, collections (old coins, newspapers, stamps, types of rocks, leaves, flowers, photographs, pamphlets), models (2-dimensional or 3-dimensional, e.g., monuments, volcanoes, still scenes), videos of rallies/haat bazaars/book fairs/any social events in their surroundings.

Twenty-first century skills-based concept: Such project-based learning can be an important model for learning, especially in the days to come. It is an important part of Twenty-first century learning approaches as well. It is essential that project-based learning is integrated in the curriculum to gain the maximum benefit of the strategy. Compared to standard curriculum, Twenty-first century skills are not as concrete and can therefore appear to be a bit difficult for educators to build in their students. Project-based learning helps educators to address this gap as it fosters the development of collaboration skills, improvement of critical thinking and creative thinking, problem-solving, transfer of learning and positive attitudes towards tasks. It also helps students develop content mastery through an authentic experience by providing opportunities to students for real-world contexts and problem-solving.

Another important benefit of the strategy is that it can foster strong classroom relationships between students and teachers. According to Hutchinson (2015), 'students who are immersed in project-based learning develop Twenty-first century habits of mind related to collaboration and communication, critical thinking, problem-solving, and self-direction'. Using this approach to learning has resulted in better retention of content knowledge, especially when students are invested in projects they find to be personally meaningful. Increasingly, we see in the 21st century that what we know is becoming less important to what we can do with what we know. Twenty-first century skills are necessary for the future of employment, education, digital citizenship and for active citizenship in the world.[6]

2. **NCF:** Issues-based learning can be an excellent tool to acquaint students with various aspects of social realities, integrate perspectives from different disciplines in investigating the causes of issues and think about relevant social action. It is also important that students learn much of the social science content by engaging with real issues in their immediate or related context. For instance, students may consider the problem of drinking water shortage in their area, which may involve engaging with questions such as: What are the available sources of water? How does water consumption differ across different parts of the region or locality? Are there

wastages that can be avoided? How is water being made accessible to all sections of society? Is there unequal distribution? What steps are being taken to purify water? How is it being made available to the poorer sections of society?

Twenty-first century skills-based concept: Problem-based learning involves students focusing on solving complex, real-world problems, often using a case study approach. Students can work in small groups to investigate, research and create solutions to problems that can have multiple solutions and methods to reach them.[7]

3. **NCF:** Conversations, discussions and debates: Conversations are extremely vital in a social science classroom since these conversations often lead to focused discussions on concepts, ideas, belief systems and value claims. Sometimes, these discussions may turn into lively debates in the classroom. It is important to encourage such debates as it provides students with the opportunity to put forth their perspectives, resolve conflicts, iron out contradictory ideas and learn from each other. However, appropriate care must be taken that such discussions and debates do not hurt the sentiments of any social group or be unfit for a school environment. Some common topics for discussion could be on climate change, diversity in clothing and

types of food as per historical and geographical reasons and practising democratic processes in schools.

Twenty-first century skills-based concept: Focus group discussions are increasingly becoming a powerful tool to gather qualitative insights from employees within an organization. When conducted effectively, such group discussions can provide invaluable feedback on a range of topics, from employee engagement and satisfaction to opinions on new initiatives and policies.[8]

Group discussions are also used by employers to assess candidates' communication skills, teamwork abilities and leadership potential. In such scenarios, candidates are asked to:

a) Understand the topic and the objective of the discussion before starting. One can ask clarifying questions if needed.
b) Listen actively to what others are saying and respond thoughtfully. Using non-verbal cues to show one's engagement in the activity is also important.
c) Be respectful of others' opinions and avoid interrupting or dominating the discussion. This encourages others to participate.
d) Communicate effectively by using clear and concise language to convey one's thoughts and ideas. It is best to avoid jargon or technical terms at the very beginning.

e) Demonstrate leadership by taking the initiative and leading the discussion if appropriate.

f) Show creativity by thinking outside the box and by coming up with innovative solutions or ideas. Using examples or analogies to illustrate one's points can be very helpful.[9]

4. **NCF:** Role plays and simulations: Role plays and simulations may help learners explore decision-making processes and find means for conflict resolution. For instance, role plays of the *gram* panchayats may be used as a method to explain the functioning of a democratic institution.

Twenty-first century skills-based concept: Simulations are increasingly being used in higher education settings. Simulation can be defined as a tool that reproduces the real-life characteristics of an event or situation. It is an educational tool or device with which the learner physically interacts to mimic real life and in which they emphasize the necessity of interacting with authentic objects.[10]

A flipped classroom model can be used in simulation. It is an instructional strategy that aims to increase student engagement and learning by having students complete readings at home and work on live problem-solving during class time. This pedagogical style moves activities, including those that may have traditionally been considered homework, into the classroom. With a flipped classroom, students collaborate in discussion (which can be online as well) or carry out research at home while actively engaging concepts in the classroom with a mentor's guidance.[11]

Thus, by simulating (imitation of a situation or process) the role of an instruction giver, students can engage in depth with the teaching-learning process and help build their confidence on the matter at hand.

5. **NCF:** Community service and field excursions: Community service is another engaging strategy in a social science classroom that not only involves concrete experiences for learning concepts from the curriculum but also enables students to develop the desired values. Students may take up various projects to work with local government agencies to acquire first-hand experience of issues and work with people in need. Similarly, field excursions are meaningful ways of engaging with the content, e.g., nature walks, heritage walks, food walks and visits to police stations, museums, post offices, planetariums and government and digital archives.

   Twenty-first century skills-based concept: Many universities are moving towards community service learning (CSL) to prepare students to become productive Twenty-first century citizens. CSL enables students to participate in, and reflect on, services that both benefit the public and also contribute to their own learning. There has been considerable research conducted on the improved student competencies, both academic and personal, resulting from following this approach.

CSL can be defined as a course-based, credit-bearing educational experience in which students:

a) participate in an organized service activity that meets identified community needs
b) reflect on the service activity in such a way as to gain further understanding of course content while having a broader appreciation of the discipline and an enhanced sense of civic responsibility.[12]

6. **NCF:** Reflective essays: Students can write reflective essays on various topics related to the curriculum. These essays can also be used by teachers to assess the extent to which students have learnt the desired concepts and skills. For instance, a reflective essay topic could be 'How will dams transform agricultural productivity in India?', 'What are the issues and opportunities of linking rivers?', 'What sustainable agricultural strategies could a region adopt if its main river turns seasonal or dries up?' or 'Is waste management and disposal the sole responsibility of municipalities and other government agencies?'

Twenty-first century skills-based concept: College admissions essays are often used by admission officers to evaluate a candidate's nature, writing skills and ability to self-reflect. The essay is an important chance for a candidate to show what she/he will add to the academic community. The college essay can turn out to be the deciding factor in an application, especially for competitive schools, where most applicants have exceptional grades, test scores and extracurriculars. Some colleges also require supplemental essays about specific topics, such as why one has chosen a specific college. Scholarship essays are often required to obtain financial assistance.[13]

With these foundational principles of the National Education Policy 2020 in mind, let us now take a look as to how we can use 21st century skills to make our young learners (grades 3,4,5) ready for the future.

Chapter 2

Twenty-first Century Skills

ANALYSE THIS.

- Once, we needed factories in all industrial countries to manufacture products. Now, you can buy a 3D printer and start making your own goods by prototyping, all in the comfort of your home.
- Once, you bought anything that your neighbourhood shopkeeper had to offer. Now, you can purchase what you want from any part of the world with just a click. On top of it, you can be an entrepreneur yourself, anywhere in the world, and can build an online store all by yourself.
- Once, a filmmaker needed an entire studio, expensive cameras and a production team. Now, anyone with a smartphone and online presence can reach millions of viewers overnight.

Do you think it is a picture of a different world than the one we grew up in? Indeed.

The growth of technology and our reliance on it have increased dramatically over the last few decades. It is both an advantage and a disadvantage, depending on the situation and one's perspective. Modern means of communication have made it easier to reach out to friends and family all over the world. However, the use of technology to assist fraudulent practices is also on the rise. Like many other elements of our lives, technology has its benefits and limitations.

Artificial intelligence (AI) has become both a boon and a bane for education. If we use it for research and analysis, then it does open up a whole world of information and facts. However, it is increasingly being used to bypass the required journey of skill accumulation by learners, which takes years to master. And as a result, there are huge numbers of computer-generated works, which lack authenticity and originality and portray a rather grim picture of where the world is heading in terms of creativity and imagination.

How will such changes in the world we live in affect the 'workability' of our learners? One thing we can say is that competition will be fiercer, change will be faster, and knowledge alone will no longer be enough.

For students preparing for the workforce, success depends on what you can create, how you adapt and how well you collaborate with others. In other words, skills that AI cannot replace. And this does not just affect learners; it affects companies, leaders and professionals who need to continuously adapt to stay ahead in the race.[14]

What are Twenty-first century skills?

The term 'Twenty-first century skills' is generally used to refer to certain core competencies, such as collaboration, digital literacy, critical thinking and problem-solving. These skills help students thrive in the world we live in and the world they will inherit.[15] In other words, these are the abilities that today's students need to have to succeed in their careers and lead successful lives.

Armstrong Pame[16]

Meet Mr Armstrong Pame, an officer of the Indian Administrative Service (IAS) 2009 batch belonging to the Manipur cadre. He is currently serving as Joint Secretary to the Government of India, Department of Higher Education, Ministry of Education (India). Born in September 1984, Pame is a recipient of several awards, including India's Most Eminent IAS Officer Award 2015 and India's distinguished IAS Officers Award 2021. Known as the 'Miracle Man', Pame has initiated the building of a 100-kilometre-long road in one of the remotest parts of the country through crowdfunding with the villagers of the area and people from different parts of the world. He is a physics (hons.) graduate from St Stephen's College, Delhi University, and has completed a Transformational Leadership Course from Oxford University and the Leadership in 21st Century Executive Education Module from Harvard Kennedy School. He is also recognized as a Young Global leader of the Class of 2018 by the World Economic Forum.

The road built by this determined, dedicated officer is famously known as the 'Peoples' Road', which connects Manipur to Nagaland and Assam.[17] But the story behind the Peoples' Road is one of great collaboration, strength and understanding. Posted in his village, as a sub-divisional officer, Pame reached out to the people to learn about their needs. This road was one of the key requirements of the people. Pame not only listened to the people but he actively took it up with his department. However, as in many cases, bureaucratic delays and hurdles delayed the effort to build this road. Pame next did something that I believe only true leaders can – he took out his own savings from his previous service, and his friends and family joined in, too. The most heartwarming part of the story is even villagers, who did not have much, enthusiastically joined in to help pool funds for the road! Pame would share, 'One ninety-two-year old man stood up and said, "Sir, I am going to give you my five month's salary, which comes to around thousand bucks, because I get around two hundred rupees a month as old age pension." One widow stood up and said, "Sir, I do not have money, but I am going to give you all the firewood that all the labourers will need for their cooking." And that's how we started the journey of something called the People's Road.'

It took over nine years of continuous hard work, and the people finally had their road in February 2013. But that is not the end! Pame returned to the village in 2020 as district magistrate and decided to talk to the government to make the road a national highway. He went to forty-eight villages in Assam and Manipur, risking his life during the COVID-19 pandemic, to talk to the people about the problem of land acquisition, which was obstructing the creation of the national highway. The people had complete trust in Pame, and he received an overwhelming amount of support, yet again! Pame observes, 'We got a funding of 3,200 crore from the Ministry of Road Transport.'[18] This 'People's Road' has now been declared as National Highway 137 by the Ministry of Road Transport and Highways.

Armstrong Pame is also a motivational speaker on various platforms, including TEDx, and speaks at corporate events, universities and other notable public events.[19]

Construction of Peoples' Road[20]

Keeping this inspiring real-life story in mind, let us look at the following list of Twenty-first century skills. Do you find any familiar skills that you came across from this study of the journey of Peoples' Road to National Highway 137?

There are THREE categories of Twenty-first century skills. They are as follows:

1. Learning skills
2. Literacy skills
3. Life skills

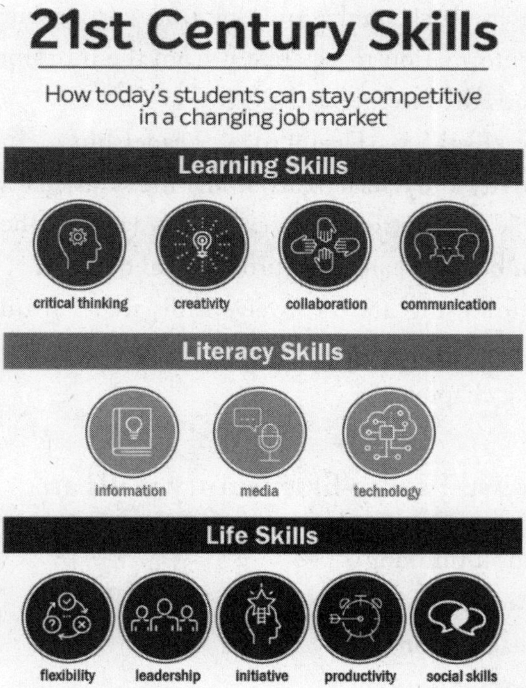

Fig, The categories of Twenty-first century skills

Each category has its own subdivisions. The Four Cs (Critical Thinking, Creativity, Collaboration and Communication) under learning skills teach students about the mental processes required to adapt and improve upon a modern work environment.

The IMT (Information, Media and Technology) under literacy skills focuses on how students can discern facts, publishing outlets and the technology behind them. There's a strong emphasis on determining trustworthy sources and factual information to separate it from the misinformation that floods the internet.

The FLIPS (Flexibility, Leadership, Initiative, Productivity and Social Skills) under life skills take a look at intangible elements of a student's everyday life. These skills focus on both personal and professional qualities.

The following are the twelve skills that fall under the above categorizations. They will be discussed in detail in the following chapters.

The twelve Twenty-first century skills are:

1. Critical thinking
2. Creativity
3. Collaboration
4. Communication
5. Information literacy
6. Media literacy
7. Technology literacy
8. Flexibility
9. Leadership
10. Initiative
11. Productivity
12. Social skills[21]

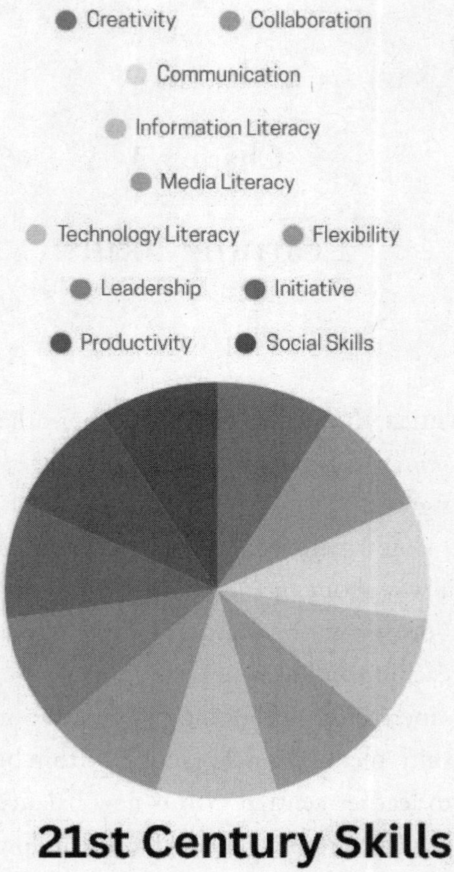

Fig: List of key Twenty-first century skills

Chapter 3

Learning Skills

BERNIE TRILLING AND CHARLES FADEL, in their book *21st Century Skills, Learning for Life in Our Times*, have shared a very insightful observation made by a teacher: 'I had to unlearn the idea that teaching was about *my* content; I had to learn it was about *their* thinking and *their* skills.'[22] This emphasis on *them*, the learners, is vital for Twenty-first century teaching and learning.

With increasing technological innovations, there is indeed a shift in educational practices – from being teacher-directed to learner-centred.[23] This new balance of Twenty-first century education is reflected in the following table:

Table 1: A New Balance[24]

Teacher-directed	**Learner-centred**
Direct instruction	Interactive exchange
Knowledge	Skills
Content	Process

Teacher-directed	**Learner-centred**
Basic skills	Applied skills
Facts and principles	Questions and problems
Theory	Practice
Curriculum	Projects
Time-slotted	On-demand
One-size-fits-all	Personalized
Competitive	Collaborative
Classroom	Global community
Text-based	Web-based
Summative tests	Formative evaluations
Learning for school	Learning for life

We remember learning about fundamental rights and duties back in our childhood. We most likely memorized them and answered questions like: *Write four Fundamental Rights guaranteed to all citizens of India.* Now take a look at the following question: *Which fundamental right has been taken away from a child who you see working in a steel factory?* (The Right against Exploitation: Article 24: Prohibition of employment of children in factories, etc. Some child labour-related acts in India:

- The Employment of Children Act, 1938
- The Factories Act, 1948
- The Plantation Labour Act, 1951
- The Motor Transport Workers Act, 1951
- The Mines Act, 1952

- The Merchant Shipping Act, 1958
- Apprentices Act, 1961
- The Bidi and Cigar Workers Act, 1966
- The Child Labour (Prohibition and Regulation) Act, 1986[25]

As you can see, the change in approach has led to a greater emphasis on critical thinking, application-based learning and encouraging problem-solving attitudes in learners. In fact, it is true that many consider critical thinking and problem-solving to be the new basics of Twenty-first century learning. Not just knowledge acquisition – the focus is on the application of the acquired knowledge. Applying skills like critical thinking, creativity and problem-solving to the content knowledge also increases motivation and improves learning outcomes.[26]

The Four Cs under learning skills can be considered to be by far the most popular Twenty-first century skills. There is widespread awareness among most educators around these skills because these abilities are thought to cater to the universal needs of any career. They, however, vary in terms of importance, depending on an individual's career aspirations and career trajectory. Let us discuss these four Cs in detail now.

The four Cs of Twenty-first century skills are:

- **Critical thinking**: Stands for finding solutions to problems
- **Creativity**: Promotes thinking outside the box
- **Collaboration**: Includes working with others
- **Communication**: Involves talking to others[27]

Table 2: Mapping the 4 C's and NEP 2020

The 4 C'S of 21st Century Skills	NEP 2020
Critical Thinking	• Emphasis on conceptual understanding • Creativity and critical thinking • Focus on regular formative assessment for learning
Creativity	• Creativity and critical thinking • Flexibility • Multidisciplinary and holistic education
Collaboration	• No hard separations between arts and sciences, between curricular and extracurricular activities, between vocational and academic streams, etc. • Respect for diversity and respect for the local context • Full equity and inclusion
Communication	• Promoting multilingualism and the power of language • Life skills • Ethics and human and Constitutional values

Critical Thinking

The monumental shift that the world has undergone – from an economy marked by Industrial Age production to that of a Knowledge Age economy is as intense as the previous shift from the Agrarian to the Industrial Age, a few hundreds of years ago. Today's Knowledge Age is driven by information, linked globally with complex networks. Thus, teaching an learning in the present age need to move away from the nuts and bolts of the factories (which, mind you, still remain and important part of our economies) and move towards a path marked with data, information, knowledge and expertise. The following Value Chains will illustrate the mentioned concept further:

Industrial Age Value Chain

Extraction → Manufacturing → Assembly → Marketing → Distribution → Products (and Services)

Knowledge Age Value Chain

Data → Information → Knowledge → Expertise → Marketing → Services (and Products)

Hence, to build expertise, there needs to be a critical analysis of the data and information provided to us. Critical thinking is one the most important qualities today's learners require.

Psychologist Robert Sternberg defined critical thinking as 'the mental processes, strategies and representations people use to solve problems, make decisions, and learn new concepts'. Education professor Michael Scriven and philosopher Richard Paul defined critical thinking as 'the intellectually disciplined process of actively and skilfully conceptualizing, applying, analyzing, synthesizing, and/or evaluating information gathered from, or generated by, observation, experience, reflection, reasoning, or communication, as a guide to belief and action'.[28]

Essentially, effective critical thinking should inspire students to solve problems and make new discoveries. Ideally, it needs to help students *figure things out* for themselves, initially with the help of teachers, and mainly when they don't have a teacher with them.[29] Critical thinking is extremely important in the long run and very essential to navigating the complex world.

Let us now take a look at a few activities that promote critical thinking and problem-solving in terms of social studies. The same activities can have multiple variations depending on the grade and age of learners in focus.

Problems in a Jar

Duration: 10–15 minutes

Instructions:

1. The teacher to put in a jar paper chits with dilemmas written on them. Students can be asked to come up to the teacher's desk and pick a chit.
2. Students to then share with the teacher and the class how she/he will solve the problem.

Variations:

1. For students who are in grade 3, the solution can be very simple. The teacher needs to include simple, direct questions in the chits.
2. For grade 4, students can be asked to work out the solution in pairs and then share the same with the class.
3. For grade 5, there can be time allotted to the students (working in pairs or in groups) to come up with a solution and present it to the class by using charts, skits, storytelling or any other form of presentation.

The difficulty levels of the questions/problems need to be grade specific, keeping in mind the abilities of the age group in focus.

The following are a few examples of such question/ problems from geography that can be used by teachers:

Geography. Topic = Seasons, Weather and Climate

Grade 3:

Q1. You really want an ice cream to cool down. What season do think you are in?

Q2. Mahesh forgot to take his umbrella to school. He is worried he might get drenched (wet), because it is the ____________ season.

Q3. It was cold in the morning, but now it feels quite warm. Today's ___________ is confusing to me!

Q4. Rima is packing colourful sweaters for her trip to Darjeeling during winter because she might get cold. Do you agree with her? Why?

Grade 4:

Q1. Two friends, Binny and Madhav, are talking over the phone and sharing their excitement over the upcoming monsoon season in India. Binny is in Kolkata (West Bengal), and Madhav is in Kochi (Kerala). Who do you think will see the monsoon arrive first – Binny or Madhav?

Q2. My aunt gave me a beautiful oak tree leaf which she found lying on her garden floor today. This is the season before winter when trees in some parts of the country shed their leaves. Which season are we talking about? Why do you think some trees shed their leaves before winter?

Q3. Hello, friends! I am going to a place this year that has hot summers and cold winters, with very little or no rain during the monsoon. What type of climate am I expecting?

Q4. My teacher told me that there is a difference between weather and climate. I wonder what that difference could be ...

Grade 5:

Q1. Lucy wrote a letter to her friend Max about the wonderful snowfall that she saw during Christmas. Lucy is from Sweden, and Max is from Australia. Max wrote back sharing his experience of Christmas in Australia, but his was a celebration without snowfall. In fact, it was warm enough for him to have iced juices that day! What is the reason behind such a difference in climate in Sweden and Australia on Christmas?

Q2. I was standing in a field on a hot summer day and saw my shadow towards the left. On which side of mine will I find the sun up in the sky?

Q3. Why do we have longer days in summer and shorter days during winter?

Q4. I love spring. But why does it come only once a year?

Teachers can help students in their quest for solutions, thus coming up with class discussions. It can be a great winding-up activity after an instructional lesson to help in both critical thinking and knowledge application.

Riddles

A riddle can be explained as a statement or question or phrase that has a veiled meaning, often put forth as a puzzle to be solved. Archer Taylor (one of America's 'foremost specialists in American and European folklore') once observed that 'we can probably say that riddling is a universal art'. He cited riddles from hundreds of different cultures, including Finnish, Hungarian, American Indian, Chinese, Russian, Dutch and Filipino sources amongst many others. In fact, many riddles and riddle themes are internationally widespread.[30]

Riddles find representation in modern literature as well. For example, in J.R.R. Tolkien's novel, *The Hobbit*, Gollum challenges Bilbo Baggins in a game of riddles in the dark tunnels beneath the Misty Mountains. The stakes are high: If Bilbo wins, Gollum will show him the way out; if Bilbo loses, Gollum will eat him!

Even when our children are absolutely safe from the Gollum, let's recreate some of his riddles to have a fun-filled activity on history using the strategy of riddles and thus ensuring critical thinking among young learners.

Asked by Gollum[31]	Asked by the Teacher
What has roots as nobody sees, Is taller than trees Up, up, up it goes, And yet never grows? **Answer:** Mountain	(Topic: Ancient Egyptians) **Grade 3** What in Egypt has steps but nobody climbs, Is taller than trees Up, up, up it goes, and is very steep? **Answer:** Pyramids
It cannot be seen, cannot be felt, Cannot be heard, cannot be smelt. It lies behind stars and under hills, And empty holes it fills. **Answer:** Dark (Darkness)	(Topic: Ancient Egyptians) **Grade 4** It can be seen, can be read, Has symbols and creatures stating intent, And temple walls it fills. **Answer**: Hieroglyphic script
A box without hinges, key or lid, Yet golden treasure inside is hid. **Answer:** Egg	(Topic: European history) **Grade 5** An era without superstitions, A rebirth of Greek and Roman, Valuable as gold, beautiful as the Mona Lisa! **Answer**: The Renaissance

The Mona Lisa *by Leonardo da Vinci*[32]

Critical thinking forms a major component of Cognitive Learning Theory. The meaning of the word 'cognition' is 'the use of conscious mental processes'.[33] It is said to encompass all aspects of intellectual functions and processes such as perception, attention, thought, imagination, intelligence, the formation of knowledge, memory and working memory, judgement and evaluation, reasoning and omputation, problem-solving and decision-making, comprehension and production of language. Cognitive processes are also known to use existing knowledge to discover new knowledge.[34]

Cognitivism is a theoretical framework for understanding the mind that gained increased currency in the 1950s. Many saw the movement as a response to behaviourism, which cognitivists said neglected to explain cognition. According to cognitivists, we have a complex physiological structure that absorbs a variety of stimuli from the environment, stimuli being the interactions that are able to produce knowledge and skills. Parents process such knowledge informally in the home while teachers process knowledge formally in school. This process of assimilating and expanding our intellectual horizon is termed cognitive development and is crucial for the teaching-learning to take place.[35]

Cognitivism suggests that we are more than just a product of our environment. We are active agents. According to Jean Piaget, understanding experiences is the way to learn. As learners understand how their thinking impacts their learning and behaviour, they are able to assert more control over it. While behaviourism suggests that learners have a passive conditioned role in learning, cognitivism states that the learners actually play a more active role.[36]

This focus on cognition is found in the Cognitive Learning Theory, which suggests that our cognitive processes have a role to play in determining knowledge and behaviour. Mental operations, such as analysing, organizing and storing, are used to understand the world around us and are thus vital for learning. In other words, Cognitive Learning Theory opines that learning is influenced by creativity.

Creativity

Now back to our discussion of the four Cs under learning skills (Twenty-first century skills). The next 'C' up for analysis is creativity.

Sir Kenneth Robinson had once observed, 'We do not grow into creativity, we grow out of it – or rather, we are educated out of it.'[37]

It is then not the lack of creativity but the lack of appreciation of creative methods and solutions that has become a major issue in our education system at large.

Why is creativity an important skill, rather, why for the 21st century? The importance of creativity as a skill essentially lies in developing the quality of innovation and adaptation among learners. This skill empowers students to see concepts in a different light, which leads to innovation and possible adaptations. In any field, whether science-based, commercial activities, humanities-based, innovation is key to the adaptability and overall success of an individual and also companies.[38]

Creative thinking has become essential for success in the 21st century. According to Daniel Pink, the skills that were important in the past (the popularly termed 'left brain skills') are still important but not enough. He suggested that the 'right brain qualities' of inventiveness, empathy and joyfulness will increasingly determine who flourishes and who struggles.

While there has been an increased creativity in education, this has not translated into practice. Education policies need to emphasize giving students and teachers a framework to help them develop creative thinking skills, spanning all disciplines and subjects.[39] The National Education Policy (NEP) of India (2020) has placed creativity and critical thinking as one of the fundamental principles that will need to guide both the education system in the country, as well as the individual institutions within it. This focus on creativity and critical thinking, the NEP states, will subsequently encourage logical decision-making and innovation.[40]

Let us see how young learners can use their creativity to approach issues that are prevalent today and have a trajectory of becoming more intense as we move on to the future.

What? So what? Now what?

Duration: 30–40 minutes

Instructions

1. Teachers to set one problem for the entire class to think about. They will need to come up with the effects of the issue set by the teacher and then find solutions on their own, using their imagination, to the problem mentioned by the teacher.
2. The problem is WHAT, the effects of the problem are SO WHAT, and the solutions offered by students are NOW WHAT.

Variations:

1. Students in grade 3 can be asked to draw, colour and use short sentences to express the solution they have in mind. This way, young learners will not only use words but also tap into their artistic side for better expression of their ideas.
2. For grade 4, students can be asked to present the solution with others in the class and also receive feedback from them.
3. For grade 5, the students can be asked to give a list of pros and cons to their solution.

The following are a few examples of *What? So What? And Now What?*

Exercises:

Civics: Grade 3

WHAT: I know a boy in my neighbourhood whose family is unable to send him to school. They say that sending him to school is too costly for them.

SO WHAT: This can result in the boy not learning how to read and write. He will also not be able to study and make friends in school.

NOW WHAT: I am going to talk to my parents and ask them to help the boy out. I will also ask my teacher for help. I can make notes from my books and give it to him on weekends. I can also, with my parents, help him do his homework and solve questions.

Geography: Grade 4

WHAT: Increasing air pollution, especially in urban areas.

SO WHAT: Numerous health hazards and illnesses are caused by polluted air. It can lead to strokes, heart disease, lung cancer and asthma among other illnesses for humans. Acid rain, ozone depletion and global climate change are some of the most serious environmental effects of air pollution.

NOW WHAT: Encourage residents of urban areas to opt for public transportation instead of private vehicles to reduce the use of fossil fuels. Talk to the community to adopt solar power panels for daily electricity needs. Distribute plant saplings and organize drives to improve plant cover in urban areas. A good start would be to help parents to garden in their own homes.

Students can collaborate with organizations dealing with environmental issues. There are numerous organizations, for example, that are combating air pollution around the globe. Help Delhi Breathe is a nonprofit environmental organization that was formed in 2015 to help end the air pollution crisis in Delhi. The organization's main goal is to educate the city's residents about the dangers of air pollution and sensitize them to devise permanent solutions to the problem. Help Delhi Breathe aims to provide accurate information to everyone in the city, encourage clean public transport and also help Delhi adopt clean, renewable solar energy.[41]

A detailed list of civil society organizations around the world and a list of their activities against pollution can be found on the United Nations Environment Programme website.

Civics: Grade 5

WHAT: Revathy lives in a small village near Chennai. She has seen that fewer of her fellow villagers are participating in the meetings of the rural local self-government – the panchayat – than before.

SO WHAT: *Gram* panchayats ensure the cooperation of the villagers in developing their community. It also trains young people to become good leaders. The panchayats also aim to end mutual conflicts and differences. All these important functions of the rural local self-government will become difficult if people do not participate willingly.

NOW WHAT: Revathy could speak to her friends in the village and together talk to their parents and family members about what could be the reason behind such reduced participation. They could also visit the sarpanch to ask for guidance. By working together, they could create awareness among the villagers. If possible, and when necessary, panchayat meetings could be done online to help villagers with access to the internet, who could thus take part in the meetings from their places of work.

The pro of this solution is that Revathy and her friends – who are the future of the country – are well aware of the importance of the panchayati system and are more likely to take part in its proceedings wholeheartedly.

However, a major obstacle to this solution is the availability of good internet connections across all parts of the villages. Sometimes, such provisions are difficult to find. This then becomes a larger issue of lack of support from effective infrastructure.

The importance of creativity is thus noble. It is not surprising that there is a strong emphasis worldwide on this particular skill. For instance, the World Economic Forum came up with an article in 2020 identifying the top fifteen skills needed for 2025. The four identified 'capabilities' required from students accruing to the forum are:

- Critical thinking/problem-solving
- Creativity
- Communication
- Collaboration

Similarly, Forbes listed the following five 'future of work' skills as vital for the future:

- Creativity
- Emotional intelligence (EQ)
- Analytical (critical) thinking
- Active learning with a growth mindset
- Judgement and decision-making[42]

Just think of little Ishaan Avasthi from *Taare Zameen Par*. Whether it's his drawing of soldiers digging trenches or his boat made of twigs and pencils, creativity is what makes us aware of our skills, even when the world around us might not yet be aware of them.

To conclude our discussion on creativity, let's quote Albert Einstein: 'Imagination is more important than knowledge. Knowledge is limited. Imagination encircles the world.'

With courage and persistence, the requisites of a creative mind, let us inspire our present and future generations to harness the power of knowledge and push for innovative solutions for even the most complex problems of the world.[43]

Collaboration

Back in 1974, the National Council of Educational Research and Training (NCERT) had released a short educational video, named *Ek Anek Ekta*. Its simple message, beautiful animation and wonderful rhythm are remembered by many even today. We learn how collaboration and unity can help us succeed even at the most difficult task.

Collaboration is getting students to work together, achieve compromises and get the best possible results from solving a problem. It may be the most challenging concept in the four Cs. But once mastered, it can help teams and companies achieve their highest goals.

The key element of collaboration is willingness. All participants have to be willing to sacrifice parts of their own ideas and adopt others to get the best results. Collaboration needs cooperation, mutual understanding and the awareness of the idea of a 'greater good'.[44]

Here is a list of classroom-friendly ideas to usher in collaboration among students, which can be applied to specific content as well.

Table 3: Fun team-building activities[45]

Activity	What it builds	How it works
Story Circle	Creativity, listening, group participation	Each student adds a sentence to build a class story, spoken or written.
Team Art Mural	Shared ownership, creativity, thematic thinking	Each group decorates part of a poster that connects to a class theme.
Hot Seat (Academic Edition)	Content review, vocabulary, quick thinking	One student guesses the term behind them based on clues from the class.

Activity	What it builds	How it works
Walk and Talk	Social bonding, active reflection	Students pair up and discuss a prompt while walking.
Rose, Thorn, Bud Check-in	Emotional awareness, reflection, connection	Students share a highlight, a challenge and something they're looking forward to.
Mystery Drawing Pairs	Active listening, communication and creativity	One student describes a mystery image and the other draws. Then they switch roles.
Would You Rather Wall Walk	Discussion, perspective-taking, movement	Students pick a corner to match their choice and discuss with the group.
Paper Chain Goals	Reflection, goal setting, class unity	Students write goals on paper strips and link them into a shared chain.

Let us apply some of these team-building activities in social studies across grades 3, 4 and 5.

Activity	What it builds	Instructions
Story Circle (Topic: The Harappan Civilization, history), grade 3	Creativity, listening, group participation	1. Teachers can assign a part of the given topic, like who were the people living in Harappan civilization? What do we know about the seals discovered from Harappan cities? What happened to the Harappans?

Activity	What it builds	Instructions
		2. Each student adds a sentence to build a discussion on the given topics by the teacher. This can be either spoken or written.
Walk and Talk (Topic: The Indus Valley Civilization, history), grade 4	Social bonding, active reflection	1. Teachers come up with a few prompts and put them on the class board. Prompts from this topic could be: What could have been the function of the Great Bath found at Mohenjo-Daro? Did the Indus Valley Civilization have contact with Mesopotamia and other parts of the world? What could be the reasons behind the decline of the civilization? 2. Students pair up and discuss a prompt while walking.
Hot Seat (Academic Edition) Topic: The Vedic Age, history), grade 5	Content review, vocabulary and quick thinking	1. Teachers to assign a few terms related to the content taught in class while one student is allowed to go for a walk in the corridor.

Activity	What it builds	Instructions
		2. Meanwhile, the rest of the students prepare a list of clues for the words given to them. For example, from the Vedic Age, such terms could be: Aryavarta, Samiti, Ashvamedha yagna, Sanyasa, guru dakshina, etc. 3. The student then rejoins the class and tries to guess the term based on clues from the class. 4. This activity needs to have multiple rounds so that multiple students can be given a chance to be in the 'hot seat' and try to guess the correct answer. It is also fun for the rest of the class, since they need to prepare clues, which makes them think critically.

Here are some guidelines for effective collaboration:

- **Clear objectives**: Before we start, we must have a clear and well-defined shared objective. Without it, achieving anything as a team is extremely difficult. Furthermore, a clear goal should be communicated to the team at all times. For successful team collaboration, a shared vision, established checkpoints, lack of hidden motives and a single objective at the end are all required.

- **Skills diversification**: A well-balanced diversity of abilities is required to divide the given work fairly and allow team members to learn from one another and improve their bonds.
- **Establish communication protocols**: It is critical for the team to have well-established communication standards to be able to communicate and collaborate.
- **Be coachable**: Michael Jordan used to say that his best skill was that he was coachable. He was like a sponge and absorbed learning. Such an attitude among all team members would facilitate team collaboration and assist team members to grow and deliver.
- **Lead by example**: When it comes to effective collaboration, the team leader should be a role model. She/he needs to create and participate by always welcoming co-creation, promoting open communication and providing time for them to develop and collaborate.
- **Give permission to lead**: It is important to remember that excellent leaders must also be good followers. The trick here is knowing when you should lead and when you should follow.
- **Trust**: When members trust one another, they work together. They truly listen to one another and presume

the best in one another here. They become transparent and even vulnerable over time.[46]

Communication

> The single biggest problem in communication is the illusion that it has taken place.
>
> – George Bernard Shaw[47]

Effective communication is one of the most underrated soft skills in many parts of the world. It is often viewed as a skill that is 'given', and as such, there might be a tendency to even take good communication for granted. But what happens if we do not communicate effectively? For companies, class projects and events in general, this can lead to failure in meeting targets, sometimes even an entire collapse of the given project, assignment and the like. This is a situation where none of the participants can clearly see the objectives they want to achieve. No one can take responsibility because nobody has claimed it.

We can say that communication, rather effective communication, can be regarded as the glue that binds people together and helps bring success to the collaborative undertakings of the participants. Without good communication skills, a candidate's educational qualities, learning skills and career aspirations will be difficult to bring forth the desired outcomes. Today, communication has become an important requirement for many companies. Effective communication has the potential to eliminate confusion in the workplace, schools, universities or any other group-based work projects. Good communication skills among students make them valuable parts of their teams, departments, and in the future, the companies that they wish to join or start. It is crucial for students to learn how to effectively convey ideas. Without understanding proper communication, students in the 21st century will lack a pivotal skill to progress in their careers.[48]

Communication, like many other skills, can be enhanced with effort, feedback, and practice. Let us take a look at a few steps that can help in effective communication:

1. Being in the habit of active listening

Active listening means being mentally and physically present in a conversation, especially while someone else is speaking. According to researchers at Utah State University, active listening builds trust and understanding. This can lead to people feeling more connected and valued. It builds confidence in the listener since the speaker feels heard.

2. Being mindful of body language and tone

Studies have found that up to 93 per cent of communication impact in certain contexts comes from non-verbal cues. So, we might say the right words, but if our tone sounds off or our body language is closed off, the message might not resonate. We can try the following to improve our non-verbal clues while conversing:

- Keeping an open posture (gestures and postures of a person that indicate approachability and openness to communication).
- Using facial expressions that match our words.
- Avoiding crossed arms or looking away.
- Speaking at a steady pace with a friendly tone.

3. Being able to speak and write clearly

We often feel that using big, high-sounding words is a requisite for good communication. However, it is actually the opposite in most cases. Shorter and simpler sentences are easier to understand and build the conversation. Research from Wylie Communications found that sentences of eight words or fewer are understood 100 per cent of the time. Now, we do not need to put a cap on the words we say or write in a sentence, but the study surely helps us to understand that using fancy words is not the solution if one is looking to improve one's communication skills.

- Using simple, direct language is effective.
- Eliminating filler words ('um', 'like', 'you know') to avoid confusion, and lack of clarity.
- Organizing thoughts before speaking or writing.

- Reading emails or messages aloud, or re-reading them, before sending.

4. Being open to feedback

Even the best communicators have their blind spots. Feedback then becomes the mirror that opens the path to improvement. It shows how others experience your messages. Feedback can also help in understanding your strengths and building confidence.

How to invite feedback:

- After meetings and conversations, we can ask, 'Was that clear?' or 'Did it make sense?'
- We can record our speaking patterns and find out whether we are talking too fast or being too quiet.
- The basic idea here is to be open to feedback and not be defensive about the suggestions received.

5. Being able to empathize

Empathy is about recognizing and respecting others' feelings. We do not need to agree all the time, but trying to understand other's points of view is important for constructive conversations. Studies reveal that people with higher emotional intelligence (which includes empathy) are considered to be more effective communicators. We can do this by:

- Listening without judgement. (For teachers, this is practised every day while dealing with students of all ages and backgrounds).
- Acknowledging feelings by observing, 'That sounds splendid!' or 'I can imagine what you are going through'.
- Adjusting our tone during tense conversations. A calming voice often works wonders in such situations.

6. Using stories and examples

Researchers from Stanford University found that people remember stories up to 22 times more than facts alone. (I can understand why I was glued to all the storytelling sessions at family gatherings now!). On a serious note, whether we are giving a presentation or explaining our point of view, sharing a short story can make our message more relatable. We can make it work by:

- Using real-life examples. This also helps us to connect with our audience.
- Sharing short anecdotes to clarify a point.
- Describing a situation that the listener can visualize.[49]

In a post titled 'Lessons in collaboration from Vallam Kali – the Kerala boat race', the author observes that the most striking aspect of the Kerala boat race is the trust among the rowers. Each paddler relies on the strength and rhythm of their teammates, knowing that no single person can win the race alone.

Similarly, trust, open communication and the ability to work as a unified force are the foundation stone for a good collaboration, whether at school, at the workplace or in the family. When teams embrace synergy, they not only complete tasks but also power through challenges and achieve remarkable results.[50]

With these tips and suggestions for effective communication, let us see how we can bring these into our social studies classroom. Like all other skills, good communication also needs practice, and what better place to do so than in our school settings?

Activity: 'Simon Says' but with a twist (for practising active listening)

We all have played a version of 'Simon Says' at some point in our life. Remember, 'Simon says to look for something blue', and off we go jumping around trying to touch a blue object in our room! Or when 'Simon says to stand up on one leg', we tried our best to do so, and the naughty ones among us will try to make the other fall! The instructions for this game are very simple: When Simon gives a command starting with 'Simon says…', the other players have to follow the instructions. If a player doesn't follow the instructions correctly, they are out of the game. The last player standing is the winner.[51] This beloved childhood game is essentially a listening game. We can use this game but include a twist. For us, Simon's directions will pertain to study material.

For instance, 'Simon says, jump twice if you agree that CE stands for Common Era,' or, 'Simon says, "Turn around once if pharaohs once ruled Egypt"' or, 'Simon says to clap your hands if Babylon was in Mesopotamia,' 'Simon says to jump and sit on the floor if you think Hiuen Tsang never visited India.' (For Grade 3, history)

Not only does the novelty of moving and jumping around increase the students' enthusiasm but the inclusion of lesson-related content makes them listen attentively to each command, thus promoting active listening. Simon might be laughing in the shadows as students hop, skip and flip over confusing facts, but hey, didn't we want learning to be fun?[52]

Activity: Sticker badges (for effective feedback)

Teachers can introduce a competition in class wherein students get to give feedback to a fellow classmate's answer, but hold on! The feedback needs to be polite, clear, without judgement and needs to have empathy. If the student giving the feedback gets to meet all the above criteria, then he/she gets a sticker badge from the teacher. There can be multiple such categories of stickers to help young learners identify their strengths and also make them understand what they need to improve upon. The activity is not just about correct answers but also the feedback given by the students to others.[53]

For instance, a student gets the following badge for being polite, clear, non-judgemental and empathetic, as well as for giving suggestions to fellow classmates.

A student gets the following badge for being polite, clear, non-judgemental and empathetic but did not give suggestions to fellow classmates.

A student gets the following badge for being polite but did not have clarity of feedback and also could not offer suggestions to fellow classmates.

Topics on which students can speak in class can be varied. For example, it can be about a story that they heard about a historical figure or the experience of visiting a historical monument like the Taj Mahal, the Mysore Palace, the Golconda Fort, etc. It can also be a sharing session on how we can use more renewable energy in school, how we can have elections for class monitor in school and other such topics from social studies. (For grades 4 and above)

Activity: Role reversal (to practise empathy and cultivate a multidimensional approach)

Engaging students in a role reversal exercise where individuals take on the perspective and experiences of someone different from themselves can be an interesting activity. This exercise promotes empathy by allowing individuals to step into someone else's shoes and gain a deeper understanding of their struggles and emotions. This also helps learners to appreciate the fact that there can be multiple perspectives in a given situation.

For instance, students can be asked to make a list of points that can be used for the following question: 'Who was a better ruler – Sher Shah Suri or Humayun?' Students can be asked to play the role of either Sher Shah Suri or Humayun and speak to the class about why he/she feels that their chosen ruler had the qualities of a ruler. But it does not end here. The same students need to change roles and come up with the same kind of observations for the other personality.

So, if I play the role of Sher Shah, I can justify my claim to power by saying, 'I established centralized rule in India,' 'I had a well-organized administration, which was strictly under my control, thus ensuring better performance,' 'I introduced military reforms to upgrade the army,' etc.

I will then need to also change my stance and come up with points justifying why Humayun was the correct option. In this role play as Humayun, such points need to be made: 'I was unable to show my capabilities before, but now I have come back stronger,' 'I did see the benefits of some of Sher Shah's administrative policies, and I continued them. This shows I think about the welfare of my people,' etc. (for grade 5, history)

Empathy is the ability to understand and share the thoughts and feelings of others. It involves putting yourself in someone else's shoes and seeing the world from their perspective.[54]

Critical thinking and problem-solving can be regarded as 'expert thinking'. Communication and collaboration as 'complex communicating', creativity and innovation as 'applied imagination and invention'. These skills, under learning skills, are considered by many as vital for not just meeting the demands of Twenty-first century work, but they are at the heart of what it takes to be a self-reliant lifelong learner.[55]

Chapter 4

Literary Skills

LITERACY SKILLS OF TWENTY-FIRST CENTURY learning can be abbreviated as IMT skills. Information literacy, media literacy and technology literacy deal with a different element of digital literacy and comprehension.

- **Information literacy** is concerned with the understanding of facts, figures, statistics and data.
- **Media literacy** involves the understanding of the methods and outlets in which information is published.
- **Technology literacy** comprises the study and understanding of the machines that make the Information Age possible.

These three skills are interrelated, and together, they help learners navigate the world we live in.[56]

With the internet increasingly becoming the defining technology for literacy and learning in the 21st century, students need to be prepared to use digital resources and mediums to become skilled, strategic readers, writers and communicators in online environments.

The scope of online literacy is broad and is constantly changing, covering a variety of 'new literacies'. It is no longer enough for students to be proficient in using search engines, blogs, wikis, social media platforms, Google Docs and other emerging technologies. Future literacy demands will likely encompass technologies that are yet to be invented.

Being proficient in using online resources adds hugely to a student's preparation in a subject, assessment, project and overall skill development. For instance, good online readers use effective strategies to:

a) Locate information to answer their search
b) Critically evaluate the usefulness (and trustworthiness) of the located information
c) Synthesize the information with their analyses to answer their questions
d) Communicate their answers to others.[57]

John McCarthy coined the term 'artificial intelligence' back in 1956. It is in the recent past that AI has become an integral part of our lives: from personal digital assistants on our mobile phones to cars routinely outfitted with smart systems that decide when to activate anti-lock brakes. Algorithms guide our plane towards its gate and determine the price of our flight ticket too. Even something as mundane and trivial as email spam filters are now increasingly powered by algorithms, which learn from scanning large quantities of email traffic.

Advanced ANI (artificial narrow intelligence) systems are widely used in all sectors and industries, including the military, manufacturing, finance and medicine. We already live amidst an AI revolution, but often, we hardly recognize it![58]

How do we then prepare our young learners to not just cope and flourish in a world driven by AI but also prepare themselves for subsequent digital, technological shifts? A mindset that is digitally oriented, aware and open to change can be the starting point for such a journey.

Information Literacy

The availability of information has been made easier than ever before. In fact, we are faced with an onslaught of information even when we are not actively seeking it. However, this availability of information also comes with chronic misinformation. Finding truth online has become a job all on its own. It is crucial that students can identify honesty on their own. Otherwise, they can get baffled by the kind of misconceptions and false information that, unfortunately, have been plaguing the world.[59]

Let us start the process of looking for authentic information from an early age so that our learners are better prepared for subsequent complexities that might come up in the future.

Activity 1: Using picture sources (for grade 3, history)

Instructions

1. The teacher has given the class a statement from history. For example: Before human beings settled in particular places, they used to move around. They needed to hunt animals for food. They also collected food from plants and trees. They were known as hunter-gatherers.
2. The teacher has also given the students a few pictures to look at.

Drawings on the walls of caves showing a hunting scene[60]

A cave painting from Bhimbetka, India, showing people riding horses holding weapons[61]

3. Students need to study the pictures and answer in their notebooks which pictures they can use to support the statement given by the teacher.

The answer needs to have sources A and B as evidence for the statement. Since source C does not show either hunting or people gathering food, it cannot be used as evidence for the given statement.

We need to note that since our young learners might not be able to analyse the trustworthiness of sources at this age, the teacher needs to come up with pictures/extracts that are from authentic sites/books.

Activity 2: Using extracts (for grade 4, geography)

Source A: The Indian Meteorological Department of the Ministry of Earth Sciences, Government of India, issued a press release on 16 May 2025. It says:

i) Heavy to very heavy rainfall accompanied by thunderstorms and lightning is likely to take place over north-east India and sub-Himalayan West Bengal and Sikkim during the next five to six days.
ii) Heavy rainfall accompanied by thunderstorms, lightning and gusty winds are likely to continue over south Peninsular India for the next five days.
iii) Heatwave conditions are likely over west Rajasthan from the 16th to the 22nd, Uttar Pradesh, Jammu and Kashmir on 16th and 17th and north Madhya Pradesh on 18th and 19th May 2025.[62]

Source B: A letter from a friend living in Italy about his thoughts on the weather conditions in India.

> 16 May 2025
>
> Hello, my friend!
>
> It has been long since I had an opportunity to write you a letter. Things have been quite busy back in school. We had our annual exams, and then we went on a class trip to Tuscany. I have to say that the weather in Tuscany is absolutely wonderful right now! What about India? I

believe it is very cold in all parts of the country given the fact that it is the month of May. Are you all wearing your sweaters and cardigans to school?

I miss being in India and hope to catch up with all my friends soon. I love it when the monsoon sets in and brings with it thunderstorms and gusty winds. I forgot when the time for the monsoon in India is. Is it in January? Or maybe March?

Nonetheless, I love our cricket matches in the rain, even when Ma scolds me for catching a cold afterwards! Hope to see all of you soon. Please take care. Goodbye for now!

Best regards
Mohit

Instructions

1. Students to go through both the sources and underline the information that they received in both sources.
2. Students then need to come up with a list of points as to what they found correct in Source A and why. The same needs to be done for Source B.
3. Finally, students can come up to the teacher and share their thoughts as to which source they felt they could trust. The teacher should ask them why they think so.

Activity 3: Find the truth! (for grade 5, civics)

Instructions

1. Teachers to write down on the board or hand out worksheets with statements/sentences on a chosen topic.
2. Students to work in pairs and mark out the sentences they feel are true.
3. Next, they discuss with one another and write down why they found some sentences true and what made them feel the others were untrue.
4. For example:[63]

Set A:

Sentence 1: A basic human right is for everyone to have access to clean, safe water.

Sentence 2: The United Nations prepared a document in 1948 – the Universal Declaration of Human Rights.

Sentence 3: Human rights can be enjoyed by non-humans and all living beings.

(Hint: Sentence 3 is untrue)

Set B:

Sentence 1: The main purpose of all governments is to protect the rights of citizens and to promote the common good.

Sentence 2: It is not the responsibility of a country's government to maintain defence and national security of the country.

Sentence 3: In a democracy, people decide how they want to be governed.

(Hint: Sentence 2 is untrue)

Set C:

Sentence 1: Rules made by a government are known as laws.

Sentence 2: The police aim to prevent crime and maintain law and order.

Sentence 3: Laws are to help keep people safe and healthy and to prevent them from being treated badly or dishonestly.

(Hint: All are true!)

Set D:

Sentence 1: People who buy and use goods and services are called consumers.

Sentence 2: Luxury goods are the goods that people buy every day and use daily.

Sentence 3: 'Consumerism' is the practice of buying less and less consumer goods.

(Hint: Sentences 2 and 3 are untrue)

Accessing, evaluating, applying and managing information well are vital for all learners. Using information sources appropriately and effectively are also skills that define Twenty-first century digital literacy.

Media Literacy

Equally important to information literacy is our next point of discussion – media literacy. Understanding how different types of media are used to communicate messages is important for effective digital literacy. How to choose from the many media choices available to us now and how to create messages in a variety of media are some of the questions that need to be answered.

What is media?

The term media refers to messages that we see, read or hear that are typically (although not always) mass-produced and intended for a mass audience using some form of technology. This includes traditional (non-digital) media, like books – including textbooks – as well as music, product packaging, maps and a wide range of other examples.

Media literacy education looks into different kinds of media – including those that have yet to be invented. Many organizations define media literacy as the ability to access, analyse, evaluate, create and act with respect to media. The basics of media literacy involve asking questions about the messages we see, read and hear. This is followed by our reflections, analyses of our own media use, our responses to media messages, and our biases. Inquiry and reflection are also vital when considering the media we create, reflecting on our production choices – whether we are creating a film, a news article or even a tweet. In this way, media literacy is all about empowering today's learners with the skills they need to navigate the world. Protecting students from 'harmful' media messages is a by-product of such literacy.

Project Look Sharp, a nonprofit, mission-driven outreach programme of Ithaca College, USA, aims to work towards media literacy, along with some knowledge and awareness about how media messages are created and how media industries work. The emphasis is on inquiry and reflection running through all those abilities. The following are some important points that the organization has listed, which media literacy must involve:

1. Learning how to use media wisely and effectively
2. Engaging in critical thinking when evaluating media messages
3. Being able to evaluate the credibility of information from different sources
4. Recognizing media's influence on beliefs, attitudes, values, behaviours and the democratic process
5. Encouraging participatory citizenship
6. Achieving greater understanding and appreciating multiple perspectives
7. Learning to produce communication and express oneself using different forms of media.

Here are a few categories of media literacy analyses and some guiding questions that help us in attaining media literacy:

Relating to:

1. **Authorship:** Who is telling this story? Who made this?
2. **Purpose(s):** Why was this made? Who is the target audience? What does this want me to do? What do they want me to think? Why would they want me to think that?

3. **Content:** What is this about? What is this saying? What does this tell me about ________? Who are the leaders/followers? Who gets helped/who are the helpers?
4. **Techniques:** What do I notice first? What do they want me to notice first? How do they get me to notice what they want? How did they make that? Where was the camera?
5. **Context:** Does this fit into any patterns I have seen before? How is this like what I already know? Where did this come from? When was this made? Is this from a long time ago or now?
6. **Credibility:** Is this telling the truth? Should I believe this? Why should I believe this? How do I know what they are saying is true? Is this a fact or an opinion?
7. **Economics:** Who paid for this? Who might make money from this? Am I trading something valuable to watch/play/read/listen to this? What does 'free' mean?
8. **Effects:** Who might be sad/happy because of this? Who might this help/hurt?
9. **Interpretations:** What does this mean? What do they think is important? What would ________ think about this? (Insert name, group, profession, etc.) How does this compare/contrast to what I already know?
10. **Responses:** How does this make me feel? Now that I know this, what do I want to do? What can I do to change the story? What else do I want to know?

11. **Follow up:** How do I know? What makes me think that? What is my evidence? How can I find out?

The concept of media literacy is comparatively new. As teachers, we might need to familiarize ourselves with the concept before we can apply it in our classrooms. The following activity is for teachers. The exercise uses the guiding questions mentioned above to help us understand where we stand when it comes to media literacy (and social studies).

Social studies-related questions:

After looking over all four sources,

1. What bias do you notice in this representation of ancient civilizations?
2. Why might certain cultures have been left out of each map/source?
3. What questions should I ask to assess the credibility of this representation of ancient history?

Here is a possible answer to a question to help you understand the process more.

Question: After looking over all four documents, what bias do you notice in this representation of ancient civilizations?

Possible answer: There are many different possible interpretations for this question. Since all media constructions contain inherent bias, the answer can be wide-ranging answers. Each observation needs to have evidence from the document to help establish the observation firmly. One bias in source 1 is towards the definition of 'civilizations'. It has only large imperial powers rather than including the many peoples, especially in the northern and southern spheres, that included long enduring hunter-gatherer cultures and subsistence farmer cultures. One bias in source 2 is that it only chooses to include civilizations 'of the Old World', thus dismissing the many civilizations of the Americas. Source 3 is biased in the choice of the phrase 'cultural stage' to differentiate different cultural choices that need not be seen as developmental (i.e., hunter-gatherers lowest to empires highest). One bias in source 4 is the very subjective determination of the 'relative power' of each 'state, nation and empire'.

Media literacy-related questions:

1. What techniques has the cartographer used to communicate the messages? (E.g., keys, colours, visual representation)
2. How credible is the information and why?
3. What aspects of cultural context are important to consider when evaluating the usefulness of these maps/ sources?

Question: What techniques has the cartographer used to communicate the messages? (E.g., keys, colours, visual representation)

Possible answer: The cartographer who made source 1 combines colour coding of peoples with a timeline to indicate both the geographic breadth and the chronological length of each civilization. The cartographer who made source 2 uses colour to indicate time periods rather than to differentiate civilizations, enabling readers to see the shift in the location of primary civilizations over the millennia. The cartographer who made source 3 uses colours to indicate what they call 'cultural stages', allowing the viewer to recognize similar 'stages' in different locations around the globe. The one who made source 4 dispenses with traditional geographic maps altogether and represents civilizations by colour and 'relative power' by horizontal spacing.

Let us look at a few activities based on the guiding questions that we need to ask to strengthen media literacy among kids.

Geography

Source A

> **Guardians of our lakes and rivers**
> This Earth Day, learn about five fascinating animals that are crucial for the health of India's water bodies and are now being pushed to the brink by human activities.

Grey-Headed Fish Eagle

A grey-headed fish eagle, in the Mudumalai Tiger Reserve

Which wetland raptor is so closely linked with fish that even its Latin name means "Fish Eater"? The answer is the Grey-Headed Fish Eagle, a medium-sized raptor seen near the rivers and wetlands of Central Indian jungles, especially tiger reserves. While larger wetland raptors like Ospreys hunt on the fly, this eagle sits patiently on a branch to spot fish before quickly diving into the water for the hunt. Over-fishing is a significant threat to its existence, as is the destruction of forests in the Western Ghats.

Smooth-Coated Otter

This aquatic mammal is intelligent, a fantastic swimmer and loves to hunt fish. The Smooth-Coated Otter is a top predator and "keystone" species of aquatic ecosystems. You can see it in clear streams and rivers across India. They live inside burrows in small groups that even hunt together. Unfortunately, due to the building of dams and pollution of water bodies, it is now listed as "Vulnerable" in the IUCN Red List.

Dugong

Dugong

The gentle, slow-moving, grass-loving "Sea Cow" is found in the coastal waters of Andamans, Tamil Nadu and Gujarat. India's only exclusively plant-eating marine mammal is a heavy grazer with a daily consumption of 30kg of its favourite seagrass. This shy mammal is a caring parent, nurturing its calves for over a year. Coastal development, which damages seagrass beds, marine plastic pollution and ship activity is a major threat to the existence of the dugong.

Indian Softshell Turtle

Indian soft-shell turtles

Weighing an impressive 40kg, the Indian Softshell Turtle is a giant. Not a fussy eater, it gobbles up fish, frogs, snails, and aquatic plants! Today, it is only seen in the waters of the Ganga Basin in northern India. Continuous hunting for meat and riverine habitat destruction have pushed it into the IUCN Red List of Threatened Species.

Northern Dancing Frog

An important indicator of clean streams, this tiny amphibian is found only in the northern Western Ghats (Sahyadris in Maharashtra). Thus, its Latin name is Uttaraghati. The entire group of dancing frogs is known for the males' footwork to catch female attention. Forest clearing, stream diversion for agriculture, and water pollution have put it on the IUCN Red List.

Instructions

Students should go through the entire source (the article from an online version of a newspaper in India) and then answer the following questions in relation to source A.

Authorship:
Q1. Who is telling this story? Q2. Who made this?

Purpose(s):
Q3. Why was this made? Q4. Who is the target audience? Q5. What do they want me to think?

Content:
Q6. What is this about? Q7. What does this tell me about India's water bodies?

Credibility:
Q8. Is this telling the truth? Q9. Why should I believe this? Q10. How do they know what they are saying is true?

Effects:
Q11. Who might be sad/happy because of this? Q12. Who might this help/hurt?

Responses:
Q13. Now that I know this, what do I want to do? Q14. What can we do to change the story?

History

Source B

In the sun's chariot

The Sun Temple in Odisha is an architectural marvel dating back to the 13th century.

The Sun Temple

Imagine a 100-foot high chariot with 24 wheels — each 12 foot in diameter — being pulled by seven horses! Yes, we are talking of the Sun Temple at Konark, Odisha. In the late 17th century, European soldiers sailing up the eastern coast of India referred to it as the Black Pagoda, as they caught a glimpse of its tower rising up from inland.

Built in the 13th century by Narsingha Deva I of the Eastern Ganga dynasty, the Sun Temple is built in the classic Kalinga style of architecture. The structure is meant to represent the journey of the Hindu Sun God Surya across the sky. The main sanctuary was topped by a shikhara (crown) that was more than 200 feet high but this was destroyed some time in the 19th century.

The beauty of the Sun temple lies in the fabulous carvings and reliefs that decorate the walls from the base to the top. Even the wheels feature intricate work of animals, creepers and flowers and human figures.

Apart from sculptures of Hindu gods and characters from mythology, the carvings show scenes from the daily life. There are friezes that narrate stories from Hindu texts. One panel has a king receiving counsel, while others depict hunting, battles, people travelling in caravans, travellers cooking on the roadside, and celebrations. Portrayals of daily life include women applying make up, drying wet hair, playing musical instruments and so on.

Over time, the temple fell into ruins. It is not clear whether this was due to natural wear and tear or damage caused by wars. Partially restored during the colonial era and after independence, the monument was listed as a UNESCO World Heritage Site in 1984.

Fun facts

1. This is one of the few temples to have written records of its planning and construction. Palm leaf manuscripts with the details written in Sanskrit but in the Odia script were discovered in 1960s.
2. The Ain-i-Akbari written by Abul Fazl in the 16th century mentions the Sun temple as prosperous and one that "astonished" visitors.
3. The Sun temple is one of Odisha's Golden Triangle: the other two being the Jaganatha temple at Puri and the Lingaraja temple at Bhubaneshwar.
4. Three types of stone went into the making of the temple: Chlorite, Laterite and Khondalite. However, none of these are found around the area. So they must have been brought from more distant places. The stones were cut and polished till the joints are barely visible.
5. Legend has it that the temple was designed to allow the rising sun's rays to fall upon the deity in the sanctum.

   Each of the 24 wheels can be used as sun dials to tell the time.

Instructions

Students to go through the entire source. Students to then answer the following questions in relation to source B.

Authorship:

Q1. Who is telling this story?

Purpose(s):

Q2. Who is the target audience? Q3. What do they want me to think? Q4. Why would they want me to think that?

Content:

Q4. What is this about? Q5. What does this tell me about Indian architecture?

Techniques:

Q6. What do I notice first? Q7. How do they get me to notice what they want?

Context:

Q8. How is this like what I already know?

Credibility:

Q9. Is this telling the truth? Q10. Is this a fact or opinion?

Interpretations:

Q11. How does this compare/contrast to what I already know?

Civics

Source C

Instructions

Students go through a few animated videos on YouTube. Students to then answer the following questions in relation to source C.

Authorship:
Q1. Who made this?

Purpose(s):
Q2. Why was this made? Q3. What do they want me to think? Q4. Why would they want me to think that?

Content:
Q4.What is this saying?

Credibility:
Q5. Is this telling the truth? Q6. How do they know what they are saying is true? Q7. Is this a fact or an opinion?

Economics:
Q8. Who might make money from this? Q9. Am I trading something valuable to watch/play/read/listen to this?

Interpretations:
Q10. What does this mean? Q11. What do they think is important?

Surrounded by multiple media choices, Twenty-first century students need to understand how to best apply the media resources available for learning to use media creations to communicate effectively, such as through podcasts, websites and audiovisual means. The Center for Media Literacy observes that the skills for mastering media literacy should provide a framework to access, analyse, evaluate and create messages in a variety of forms. Such skills will also help in building an understanding of the role of media in society and develop the essential skills of inquiry and self-expression.

Technology Literacy

Today's 'digital natives', 'netizens', are considered to be 'bathed in bits' from birth, clutching remote controls, laptop cursors and cell phones from an early age.

But using these tools well for learning is another story. There are multiple international standards that give us guidelines for the educational use of technology, created for students, teachers and administrators. Examples of these are ISTE – International Society for Technology in Education, UNESCO.[64]

Technological literacy or technology literacy can be defined as the ability to use, manage, understand and assess technology.[65]

Technology literacy gives students the basic information they need to understand what gadgets perform what tasks and why. This understanding removes the intimidating feeling that technology tends to have. The skill of technology literacy also unmasks the high-powered tools that run today's world. It goes a step further to teach students about the machines involved in the Information Age. As computers, cloud programming and mobile devices become more important to the world, we need more people to understand those concepts and apply them effectively.[66]

Experts at UNESCO (United Nations Education, Scientific and Cultural Organization) believe that to bring technology literacy to students throughout the world, educators need opportunities to use technology in every aspect of their teaching. The more learners are familiar not only with learning about technology but learning *with* technology, the more they will be prepared to use technology to improve their lives.

In 2016, UNESCO came up with a detailed plan on how teachers can show technology literacy in their classrooms when providing ICT (information, communication and technology) education. Teachers will need to:

- Describe and demonstrate the basic tasks and uses of word processors, such as text entry, editing text, formatting text and printing. They also need to describe and demonstrate the purpose and basic features of presentation software (like PowerPoint presentations) and other digital resources.
- Describe the purpose and basic function of graphic

software. They will also need to use graphic software packages to create a simple graphic display. (We will use Canva in our discussions.)

- Be aware of the internet and know its uses. Teachers need to be able to describe how a browser works and use URLs to access websites and use search engines.
- Create an email account and use it for a sustained series of email correspondence. Teachers to also use common communication and collaboration technologies, such as (email), text messaging, video conferencing, web-based collaboration and social environments.
- Use networked record-keeping software to take attendance. It can also be used to submit grades and maintain student records.
- Locate and use software and web resources to bring in accuracy and alignment with curriculum standards. And also to match them to the needs of specific students.[67]

Let's say, as a teacher, you are planning to teach a lesson and you need to use the above-mentioned directives and guidelines by UNESCO on technology literacy. The following could be steps that you can take to create, deliver and assess your lesson in your classroom, including ICT (information, communication and technology) at all levels.

Step 1: Creating your own study material using Word.

Using a Word document, teachers can come up with their

own study materials. Information can be typed, copied and then pasted from another source; pictures can be added too. With the use of other features like shapes, word box, watermark, page borders, etc., one can make the document more interesting. Search engines like Google and Firefox help in searching the internet for related content. The document can be printed and handed over to students or uploaded as a soft copy on common sharing platforms, emailed to students, etc.

Step 2: Using PowerPoint to present

Teachers can create slides on PowerPoint with the same information from the Word documents or create new resources using PowerPoint. When we present these PowerPoint presentations (PPTs) on screen in class (or through a projector), we make the lesson even more visually accessible to children. The slides in the PPT can have texts, pictures, videos, cartoons, etc.

Step 3: The use of graphic software

Additionally, use graphic software like Canva. Such mediums usually have a wide range of design and editing options that make presentation, even documentation, very attractive.

Step 4: Use of the internet

With the above steps, we are already aware of the importance of the internet and the search engines available to us. By pasting a URL onto a search engine, we can easily find a page that has been given to us in the form of a link. (A uniform resource locator (URL) is a reference to a resource that specifies its location on a computer network and a mechanism for retrieving it.)

Step 4: Using emails, learning management systems/ platforms and video conferencing

Google and Outlook are some of the popular sites for creating email accounts. Learning management systems/ platforms like Toddle and Managebac are very useful in keeping a record of attendance, uploading marks, resources, evaluation, sharing feedback, etc. The materials created and presented in the previous steps can be uploaded on these sites as well. Video conferencing applications like Zoom, Google Meet, Microsoft Teams, etc., are extremely helpful in online conferences, classes, webinars, etc,

As a result, students can adapt to the world more effectively. They can play an important role in its evolution and guide its future.

But to truly round out a student's Twenty-first century skills, they need to learn from a third category, one that influences them personally as well as professionally.

Step 5: Using the web for accuracy and alignment with curriculum standards

The internet is a humongous place when it comes to finding resources and tools. It has enough and more to offer when it comes to searches for aligning our teaching-learning with the specified curriculum standards and qualities.

Step 6: Using technology for evaluation

There are multiple digital tools available for online evaluation. Online quizzes, crosswords, Google Classroom, etc., can be used for formative assessments. Online examination websites like Exam.net help in online assessment as well.

For students, the following guidelines can be useful to achieve and maintain technology literacy:

1. To use technology as a means to research, organize, evaluate and communicate information.
2. To be aware users of digital technologies, communication/networking tools and social networks. These mediums can be used to access, manage, integrate, evaluate and create information that will help in contributing constructively towards a successful knowledge economy.
3. To apply a fundamental understanding of the ethical and legal issues surrounding the access and use of information technologies and technology in general.

The following segment tries to provide a few ways by which teachers can help young learners navigate the digital world, which, unfortunately, does not always follow community-approved language and practices.

What should you do when someone uses mean or hurtful language on the internet?

As kids grow, they will naturally start to communicate more online. But some of what they see could make them feel hurt, sad, angry or even fearful. Teachers can help students in building empathy for others and in learning strategies that they can use when confronted with cyberbullying.

- Children should understand that it's important to think about the words we use because everyone interprets things differently.
- They need to identify ways to respond to mean words online. Using the STOP technique from an early age can help in dealing with stressful situations.
- Decide what kinds of statements are okay to say online and which are not.

The STOP technique to battle stress for students:

1. **Stop** whatever it is that you are doing right now.
2. **Take a deep breath**. If you are particularly stressed, you can prolong this step to calm your nervous system.

3. **Observe yourself**. How does your body feel? Check in whether your body feels tense. Notice which parts of the body are tense. How does your mind feel? Notice what thoughts are looping through your brain.
4. **Proceed**. You can get back to what you were doing with a new awareness of what is going on within you, and hopefully, with a more balanced nervous system.

The STOP technique and similar methods are powerful because they allow one to dissolve stress, rather than trying to control its source.

Stressful circumstances are an inevitable part of life, and unfortunately, daily stress levels are on the rise globally. Developed by mindfulness teacher Jon Kabat-Zinn, the STOP method tries to relieve stress by centring oneself in the present moment.

The main idea discussed above revolves on the keywords 'empathy' and 'interpretation'. Let us look at an activity relating to social studies that can help build these qualities in young learners.

Empathy – to imagine the feelings that someone else is experiencing

Interpret – to understand something based on our point of view

Activity: Same idea, new situation

Instructions

1. Students to study the concept they have learnt from a given source.
2. Next, they will need to apply the concept to a new situation (one that has been instructed by the teacher).

For instance:

- **Part 1:** The concept/idea in the source below (source A) is one of empathy. Students need to write in a few lines why and how the source talks about empathy.
- **Part 2:** Students to use the hints given in this part to write about empathy using the facts mentioned.

Source A: The Gift of Friendship

Chapter 1: A New Beginning

Arjun was a bright-eyed, lively ten-year-old boy, always ready for an adventure. He loved the outdoors. The sound of rustling trees, the feel of soft earth under his feet, and the distant call of birds. His family had recently moved to a small town nestled between green hills and thick groves of neem and mango trees. Arjun couldn't wait to explore. One sunny morning, he stepped out to walk around the neighborhood, hoping to get a feel for this new place. As he wandered past rows of houses and small tea stalls, he noticed a group of children playing in a nearby colony ground. With curiosity and hope in his heart, Arjun headed toward them, wondering if this might be the beginning of something special.

Chapter 2: The First Encounter

As Arjun approached, the children paused and looked his way. One of them, a girl with kind eyes and a cheerful face, walked over to him. Her name was Meera. She smiled and introduced herself with warmth and ease. Arjun felt his nervousness melt away as Meera invited him to join their game of kho-kho. Soon, they were running, laughing, and talking like old friends. In between breaks, Arjun and Meera discovered they had a lot in common. They both loved stories of faraway lands, climbing trees, and watching insects go about their secret lives. By the end of the evening, a strong bond had begun to form, stitched together with laughter and shared joy.

Chapter 3: Adventures Unfold

In the days that followed, Arjun and Meera became nearly inseparable. Every afternoon turned into an adventure, whether it was searching for chameleons in the school playground, racing paper boats in the rain-filled drains, or making forts out of old bedsheets on the terrace. They talked about everything: their dreams, the things they were scared of, and all the wild ideas that filled their heads. One Sunday, while exploring a part of the local hillock they hadn't been to before, they stumbled across a small cave-like hollow filled with old bangles, broken toys, and shiny stones. It looked like someone's secret hideout. Inspired, they drew a treasure map and began their own quest, their imaginations running free as their friendship grew deeper.

Chapter 4: Facing Challenges Together

Not every day was easy. Like all friends, Arjun and Meera sometimes argued. They had moments when they misunderstood each other or needed space. But each time, they found their way back. They learned how to say sorry, how to forgive, and how to truly listen. One stormy evening, when the power went out and thunder rumbled outside, Arjun felt uneasy and alone. Then came a knock on the door. There stood Meera, holding a small lantern and a steel dabba of hot pakoras. She sat with him through the rain, listening quietly, offering comfort without needing to say much. In that quiet moment, Arjun realized something important: real friends show up, even when it's hard.

Chapter 5: The Power of Friendship

Time moved on, and Arjun and Meera grew older, but their friendship remained steady. They had woven a thousand memories together, stargazing on the terrace during power cuts, whispering secrets during school functions, and encouraging each other through exams and competitions. They celebrated each other's wins and stood together through disappointments. One evening, they sat by the edge of a small lake just outside town, their feet dangling over the water as the sky turned shades of orange and gold. Arjun turned to Meera and said softly, "I'm really lucky you're my friend." Meera reached out and took his hand. "So am I," she replied, her smile full of affection. And as the breeze stirred the water, their friendship remained a quiet strength, guiding them through childhood and beyond. It reminded them, always, that true friendship is a gift that grows deeper with time.

Part 1: Write in your own words why and how this story talks about empathy.

Part 2: Using the facts (hints) given below, can you come up with a short paragraph on empathy?

Fact 1: 'In the Buddhist Pali Canon, the story of the Buddha's enlightenment is a powerful example of empathy. The Buddha was meditating under a Bodhi tree when he realized the suffering of all beings. This realization led him to dedicate his life to helping others overcome their suffering.'

Fact 2: 'Do not judge, for you will be judged.' – Buddha. Judging others reflects our own biases and prejudices, leading to misunderstandings and conflicts.

Let us repeat the same exercise for the next source.

Source B: The True Nature of Bhura Bhediya

Chapter 1: The Whispering Grove

In a peaceful village nestled beside the edge of the Whispering Grove, a group of adventurous children lived for stories and surprises. They called themselves the Jungle Jasoos Gang, a name that reflected both their mischief and their unity. Among them was Anaya, with curls that refused to stay down and questions that never ended. There was Kabir, whose imagination could turn an ordinary afternoon into an epic, Saanvi, always smiling and generous, and Rohan, who used a wheelchair but never let that slow his spirit. Their village was a burst of life with flowering gulmohar trees, the scent of jasmine in the air, birdsong floating across tiled rooftops, and aunties gossiping at tea stalls.

But the grove that bordered the village carried an air of mystery. Stories of the Bura Bhediya, a fearsome creature wrapped in shadows, circulated among the elders. Some said he snuck through the trees at night, causing trouble just for fun. Others swore he was cursed. Still, no one dared to go too close. But the Jungle Jasoos Gang was different. They were full of curiosity and a touch of daring. One warm afternoon, as sunlight filtered through the neem and peepal leaves, the children stood at the grove's edge.

"Let's find out if this Bura Bhediya is really as scary as they say," said Kabir, his eyes gleaming. The others nodded, a shiver of excitement running through them. "Remember," said Rohan, smiling calmly, "being brave doesn't mean you're not scared. It means you go anyway." His words gave the group courage. Together, they stepped into the forest, where the wind carried whispers through the trees and every rustle of leaves felt like a secret waiting to be told.

Chapter 2: The Meeting

The deeper they went, the stranger everything felt. The rustling around them grew louder, and the shadows deepened. Then, from behind a clump of tall grass, a huge figure appeared. It was him. The Bura Bhediya. His fur was a mix of browns and greys, and his eyes gleamed like polished stones. The children froze, expecting a snarl, but instead, the creature whimpered.

"Please, don't run," he said in a low, gentle voice. "I won't hurt you."

The children blinked, startled. "You… you can talk?" Kabir asked, unsure whether to be afraid or amazed.

"Yes," the wolf said quietly. "But I am not the monster people say I am. A chudail once cursed me, twisting my form and my story. She feeds on fear. Because of her spell, I've been stuck like this for years, feared by everyone."

Anaya stepped forward, her voice full of kindness. "How can we help you?"

The wolf looked at her, hope flickering in his eyes. "You must find the Moonlit Rose. It only blooms deep in the grove on the night of the full moon. At dawn, its petals can break the spell."

"Then we'll find it," said Saanvi, determination lighting her face.

"But be warned," the wolf added, "the chudail will not let you succeed easily." The children nodded, their mission clear. They were not just playing anymore. This was real.

Chapter 3: Tests of Courage

With the moon rising behind them, the Jungle Jasoos Gang pushed forward into the forest's heart. The trees grew taller and denser, their roots curling across the ground like sleeping snakes. The air smelled of damp soil and pine. Rohan carefully guided his wheelchair over the uneven ground, never complaining. "Let's stick together," he said. "We're strongest when we're side by side."

Soon, the trail split into two paths. One was dark and thick with thorns. The other led to a clear stream sparkling in the moonlight. "Which way should we go?" Kabir asked.

"We shouldn't pick the easier path just because it's bright," Anaya said thoughtfully. "But we also need to be wise."

"Let's check the stream first," Saanvi suggested. "We might find a clue."

As they neared the water, the sound of the stream calmed their nerves. But suddenly, a loud growl cut through the night. From the bushes stepped a huge bear, its eyes sharp and wary.

The children stood frozen. But Rohan rolled slightly forward, hands steady on his wheels. "We're not here to fight," he said calmly. "We're looking for the Moonlit Rose to help the Bura Bhediya."

The bear frowned. "That beast? He is dangerous."

"No," Anaya insisted, stepping beside Rohan. "He's under a curse. We want to help him, not fear him."

The bear paused, sniffing the air. Then, slowly, it nodded. "If that's true, I won't stop you. But the chudail is near. She'll sense what you're trying to do."

With a deep breath of relief, the children thanked the bear and continued along the stream. As twilight melted into night, they reached a clearing bathed in soft moonlight. Wildflowers filled the space, glowing under the stars.

With the moon rising behind them, the Jungle Jasoos Gang pushed forward into the forest's heart. The trees grew taller and denser, their roots curling across the ground like sleeping snakes. The air smelled of damp soil and pine. Rohan carefully guided his wheelchair over the uneven ground, never complaining. "Let's stick together," he said. "We're strongest when we're side by side."

Soon, the trail split into two paths. One was dark and thick with thorns. The other led to a clear stream sparkling in the moonlight. "Which way should we go?" Kabir asked.

"We shouldn't pick the easier path just because it's bright," Anaya said thoughtfully. "But we also need to be wise."

"Let's check the stream first," Saanvi suggested. "We might find a clue."

As they neared the water, the sound of the stream calmed their nerves. But suddenly, a loud growl cut through the night. From the bushes stepped a huge bear, its eyes sharp and wary.

The children stood frozen. But Rohan rolled slightly forward, hands steady on his wheels. "We're not here to fight," he said calmly. "We're looking for the Moonlit Rose to help the Bura Bhediya."

The bear frowned. "That beast? He is dangerous."

"No," Anaya insisted, stepping beside Rohan. "He's under a curse. We want to help him, not fear him."

The bear paused, sniffing the air. Then, slowly, it nodded. "If that's true, I won't stop you. But the chudail is near. She'll sense what you're trying to do."

With a deep breath of relief, the children thanked the bear and continued along the stream. As twilight melted into night, they reached a clearing bathed in soft moonlight. Wildflowers filled the space, glowing under the stars.

Chapter 4: The Rose in the Moonlight

In the center of the clearing, something shimmered, more radiant than anything they had ever seen.

"There it is!" Saanvi cried. "The Moonlit Rose!"

Perched atop a small mound, the rose glowed silver and blue, its petals swaying even without wind. The children approached with reverence. Anaya reached out and gently plucked a few petals. Just then, a sharp wind howled through the trees, and a figure emerged from the shadows.

The chudail.

Her cloak rippled with darkness, her eyes burning cold. "You little fools," she hissed. "You think you can steal my rose?"

Fear rose in their chests, but Rohan tightened his grip on his wheels. "We're not stealing. We're setting things right."

The chudail laughed, the sound harsh as clashing cymbals. "You're just children!"

"Children who aren't afraid to do what's right," Saanvi answered firmly. "The Bura Bhediya doesn't deserve your curse."

The chudail's eyes narrowed. "You challenge me?"

"Yes," said Kabir, stepping forward. "We're not alone. We believe in each other, and we believe in the truth."

Their voices united, steady and strong. They had come too far to turn away now.

Chapter 5: The Strength of Friendship

Furious, the chudail raised her arms. A storm whipped through the clearing, leaves flying, dust stinging their eyes. The children held on to each other.

"We have to stand strong," Rohan shouted. "Together!"

They began to chant, words rising like a song. "We believe in courage! We believe in friendship! We believe in the good!"

A light burst from their circle, golden and warm, pushing back the chudail's fury. She shrieked, her form twisting as the light surrounded her. Then, with a flash, she vanished, her curse shattered.

The grove quieted. The wind stopped. The moon shone brighter than ever.

"We did it," Anaya whispered.

They turned to the rose, its petals now glowing even brighter, as if celebrating their bravery. With care, they gathered the remaining petals and began the journey back.

Chapter 6: The New Day

When they returned to the clearing where the Bura Bhediya waited, dawn was just beginning to light the sky. The wolf stood still, eyes wide.

"Did you find it?" he asked.

"We did," said Saanvi, her smile steady. "And we faced her."

As the petals were sprinkled over him, a golden glow surrounded the wolf. Slowly, his form changed. Fur gave way to skin, and claws became hands. Standing before them now was a man with gentle eyes and a kind face.

"Thank you," he said, his voice full of emotion. "You have done what even the bravest warriors could not."

The children beamed. "You're not the Bura Bhediya anymore," Kabir said with a laugh.

"No," the man replied, smiling, "just a friend who was lost for a long time."

Word of the children's adventure spread through the village, not as a tale of monsters, but as a story of compassion and courage. The man became part of the village, helping people see that every story has layers, and that kindness can break even the strongest curses.

The Jungle Jasoos Gang, now known as the village's young heroes, had learned that bravery isn't about being fearless. It's about choosing love over fear, again and again.

And in the heart of the Whispering Grove, where once there had been fear, there was now joy, laughter, and the gentle rustle of trees sharing a new story.

Part 1: Why was the Bhura Bhediya misinterpreted?
What is the truth of Bhura Bhediya?
What are the different types of interpretations we found in the story about Bhura Bhediya and also the Jungle Jasoos Gang?

Part 2: Using the facts (hints) given below, can you come up with a short paragraph on the different interpretations of the theme: voting age for voters?

Fact 1: 'The youth of any country may offer different priorities for the future than older voters, they will one day be in charge of the country. Voting helps them learn how the civic process works in society...' As such, the voting age should be lowered.

Fact 2: 'With all the time pressures present on the average 16-year-old, from school to work to athletics and everything in between, they may not have enough time to thoroughly study the critical issues up for debate in an election. Having them guess who is a better candidate is not the same as understanding the issues through discussion.' As such, the voting age should not be lowered.

Fact 3: Voting age should not be the focus of our discussion. It does not matter. Whether it is sixteen or eighteen years old, voters need to be educated and aware of the needs of the country. So, a discussion on voter education is way more important than the voting age debate.

How do digital citizens take responsibility for themselves, their communities, and their world?

Teaching digital citizenship to young learners is all about helping kids think beyond themselves and recognize the ripple effects of their actions. Personal responsibility is important, but understanding their responsibilities to *others* can help children unlock new ways to learn and connect with their communities and even change those communities for the better.

Objectives

- To examine both in-person responsibilities and online responsibilities.
- To describe the Rings of Responsibility as a way to think about how our behaviour affects ourselves and others.
- To identify examples of online responsibilities to others.

Activity: Rings of Responsibility

Part 1: Teachers need to have a bucket of water and a coin ready with them for the first phase of the activity. Then, teachers should ask the students to gather around the bucket and watch the teacher drop a coin into the bucket full of water and watch the concentric circles grow.

Teachers should explain how dropping the coin on a part of the bucket created rings in the water throughout the bucket. Similarly, our actions and behaviour need to be our responsibility because it creates such rings or ripples in the community, just like the coin did in the bucket of water.

Part 2: Teachers to show a video on the Rings of Responsibility.

Teachers to now invite students to respond. Through class discussions, there needs to be a clarification of the point that each ring represents a person or group we all are responsible to (ourselves, our community and our world) and that being responsible to someone means that we think about how our actions will impact them – both in-person and online.

Discuss the terminology of each of these rings:

Self: The centre ring represents the responsibilities we have to ourselves, such as keeping ourselves safe and healthy.

Community: The middle ring stands for the responsibilities we have to our community, including the people we know and interact with on a regular basis. This can include both friends and family. But it can also include people we do not know well but with whom we interact (e.g., grocery store clerks, a friend in an online gaming community, etc.).

World: The outer ring stands for our responsibilities to the larger world. This would include people we do not know but whom our actions might affect.

Phase 3: Students to help the teacher draw three concentric rings (just like the one in the picture) and name them accordingly (Self, Community, World). Following this, teachers to direct students to stand outside the physical Rings of Responsibility that they have marked in the classroom. If space is an issue, teachers can also designate corners or areas of the classroom to represent the three rings.

As the teacher reads out each statement, students to move silently to stand inside the ring they think best fits with that statement. For example, if the teacher said, 'I never tell anyone my full name online,' students could walk to the centre ring – Self – because that is a way by which we can protect our privacy.

Teachers to read out the following statements, pausing after each one so that the students have time to move around.

If time permits, there could be a discussion and reflection session when students have different answers. Some examples may fit into multiple rings.

- I only use apps and websites that are okay for someone my age. (Self)
- I never share things about my friends that they would not want other people to know. (Community)
- I do not post or share information online if I am not sure that it is true. (World)
- I treat others with respect, in person or online. (Community or World)

Students to return to their seats and write in what they understand as 'My Rings of Responsibility' and use examples of statements they think need to be included in the teacher's list. They can use crayons, colour pencils or markers in their work. The activity can be concluded by inviting the students to share their answers with the rest of the class.

Let us take this concept and apply it to social studies. The following activity will help us to incorporate the 'Rings of Responsibility' in our civics lessons by focusing on key terms:

- **Community** – a group of people who share the same interests or goals
- **Responsibility** – a duty you have to yourself or others

Activity: Fishbowl, modified

Instructions

1. A fishbowl discussion requires a circle of chairs (the fishbowl) and enough room around the circle for the remaining students to observe what is happening in the fishbowl.
2. For our exercise, we will need a few chairs in the middle (i.e., the fishbowl). For our convenience, we will call this innermost circle 'Self'. Two large concentric circles surrounding the 'Self' will be called 'Community' and 'World'. (Just like the 'Rings of Responsibility')
3. A topic needs to be set by the teacher. Fishbowl discussions are most effective when students have had a few minutes to prepare ideas and questions in advance. (For us, the topic could be: The Importance of Democracy)
4. The students sitting on the chairs, in the fishbowl (the 'Self' circle), to first discuss the topic from their perspectives. For example, prompts for discussion on the importance of democracy for the self can be how it gives me (the voters) a say in the administration of my own country, etc. The idea is to generate as many points of view as possible while the students in the outer two circles observe and listen to the discussion.
5. The teacher then announces, 'Students of the "Self" circle to move out. Students of the "Community"

circle to take their place on the chairs in the fishbowl.' The students now in the fishbowl first share their observations of the 'Self' group and then discuss the topic from their perspective. For example, prompts for discussion on the importance of democracy for the community can be how it gives community decision-making power. Sometimes, this can lead to a segment of the community disagreeing with another on what kind of reforms should take place. And once again, the students in the outer circle (the 'World') observe and listen to the discussion of the members of the fishbowl.

6. Lastly, the teacher announces, 'Students of the "Community" circle to move out. Students of the "World" circle to take their place on the chairs in the fishbowl.' The students now in the fishbowl first share their observations of the 'Community' group and then discuss the topic from their perspective. For example, prompts for discussion on the importance of democracy for the world can be how and it what ways the world as a whole can benefit from the system of democracy. Will there be less wars? Or are there any drawbacks to this system? The students who have moved out will be the audience for the discussion of the members of the fishbowl.

This activity might take preparatory lessons for the teacher to make the students clear about their roles in the exercise.

But once implemented, this exercise can show the students how interconnected we are as citizens, as community members, as inhabitants of this world. They will learn the responsibility of not just sharing their perspectives politely and constructively but also being responsible enough to prepare and implement this exercise. It makes the students learn multiple concepts and skills at once.

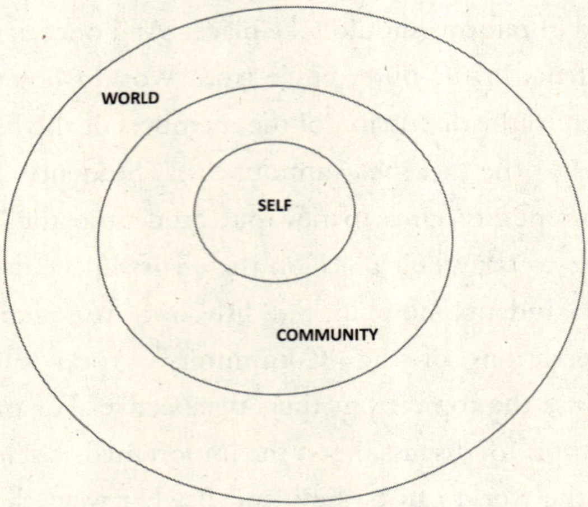

Diagram to explain the above activity

Chapter 5

Life Skills

Live in the sunshine, swim the sea, drink the wild air.

— Ralph Waldo Emerson[68]

THE CONCEPT OF LIFE SKILLS varies greatly since it depends on social norms and community expectations. However, we can say that those skills whose function is to ensure well-being and help individuals develop into active and productive members of their communities can be considered as life skills.

These skills help in developing abilities for adaptive and positive behaviour that enable humans to deal effectively with the demands and challenges of life. This concept is also known as psychosocial competency.[69]

Psychosocial competency refers to a person's ability to retain mental health and exhibit it through adaptive and good behaviour when engaging with others, his or her culture and surroundings.[70]

The development of life skills (psychosocial competency) aids people in their daily lives by allowing them to:

- Find fresh ways to think about problems and solve them.
- Recognize the consequences of their behaviour and teach them to take responsibility for their actions instead of blaming others.
- Build confidence in speaking abilities, as well as in group teamwork and cooperation.
- Analyse options, make sound judgements and comprehend why they make specific decisions.
- Develop a stronger feeling of self-awareness and gratitude towards others.[71]

Abbreviated as the FLIPS, the life skills commonly associated with Twenty-first century teaching-learning pertain to not just the personal life of an individual, but they are also an integral part of all professional settings.

The five Twenty-first century life skills are:

1. **Flexibility**: The ability to deviate from plans, if needed, to reach the greater objective.
2. **Leadership**: The much-needed source of motivation for individuals, teams and companies to accomplish a goal.

3. **Initiative**: The ability to start projects, create strategies and plan.
4. **Productivity**: The capability needed to maintain efficiency in an age of distractions.
5. **Social skills**: Meeting and networking with others for mutual benefit.

Together, the five life skills help ensure that a person can lead a successful and independent life, both personally and professionally.[72]

In 1999, the World Health Organization identified the following as the core areas of life skills:

- Decision-making and problem-solving
- Creative thinking and critical thinking
- Communication and interpersonal skills
- Self-awareness and empathy
- Assertiveness and equanimity
- Resilience and coping with emotions and stress.

UNICEF listed similar skills and related categories in its 2012 report.

The interplay between skills is what produces powerful behavioural outcomes. For example, decision-making often involves critical thinking ('What are my options?') and values clarification ('What is important to me?'), emotional intelligence ('How do I *feel* about this?). Life skills can be considered as products of synthesis. Many skills are developed simultaneously through practise, like humour, which allows a person to feel in control of a situation and make it more manageable in perspective. This also allows the person to release fears, anger and stress and achieve a qualitative life.[73]

Flexibility

> In times of change learners inherit the earth, while the learned find themselves beautifully equipped to deal with a world that no longer exists.
>
> – Eric Hoffer[74]

Flexibility is someone's ability to adapt to changing circumstances. This is perhaps one of the most challenging qualities to learn for students because it is based on two uncomfortable ideas:

1. My way is not always the best way
2. I have to know and admit when I am wrong

That is a struggle for a lot of young learners (adults too!), especially in an age when you can access any bit of information at the drop of a hat.

Flexibility thus requires one to show humility and accept that one will always have a lot to learn – even with years of experience.[75]

With a focus on the skill of flexibility, learners should be able to:

1. Adapt to a variety of roles, responsibilities, schedules and contexts.
2. Work effectively in an atmosphere of ambiguity and changing priorities.

Students are advised to be flexible and incorporate feedback effectively. While dealing with praise, setbacks and criticism, they need to have a positive outlook. They need to understand, negotiate and balance diverse views and beliefs. This way, they will be able to reach a workable solution, particularly significant in multicultural environments.[76]

Flexibility should not be seen as a weakness; in fact, it is the polar opposite of that. It is the strength that a flexible person has that allows the person to move while remaining upright with eyes on the prize. The ability to quickly analyse what is going on and make adjustments on the go is critical to success.[77]

Take for example the concept of making buildings earthquake-proof. Reinforcing a building's structure can make it flexible to sudden jolts caused by earthquakes. Shear walls, cross braces, diaphragms and moment-resisting frames are central to reinforcing a building.[78]

The core idea here is to be flexible and not break when faced with sudden changes.

Activity: Round Robin

Round robin is an interactive and inclusive classroom activity that can be used by teachers to teach concepts informally. Instead of the usual four or five students contributing to the class discussion or question and answer rounds, the round-robin strategy includes every student in the class. It needs students to brainstorm ideas on a given topic. Members of the group take turns answering a question with the use of a single word, phrase or short statement. Students share their opinions one at a time until everyone has had a chance to speak. Hence, round robin is a fantastic technique to make learning activities in the classroom more enjoyable and inclusive.

For our goal – to use the strategy of round robin – we will include a slight modification to the game. The students in each group take turns answering a question. They will also be asked to think of an opposing stance to the one they have discussed, thus making them **flexible to change**. The following instructions will make it clear:

Duration: Approximately 40 minutes

Instructions

1. The ideal way to start implementing the round-robin strategy in the classroom is to think about an issue teachers want students to talk about. An example

from social studies could be 'The importance of not modifying nature'.

2. Next, the teacher needs to decide the number of desks in the classroom, depending on the number of questions or sub-topics students will be asked to address.
3. With the help of students, the desks need to be arranged in a way that allows the conversation to flow well and so students can simply walk from one desk to another. There needs to be enough space between the desks so that groups are not distracted by the other groups.
4. Teachers to assign one sub-topic or question related to the theme of discussion for each table. This could be done by simply writing the question or sub-topic on paper and pasting them on each table. Teachers then distribute discussion sheets to each table and choose one person as the group's leader to summarize the discussion and jot it down on the discussion sheets.
5. Each group answers according to a set time (could be 4–5 mins). Groups can be given 'talking tokens' so that when it is their turn to speak, each kid must turn in a token, thus contributing to the overall discussion of the group. This helps in the progress of the group discussion.
6. After each group has discussed each sub-topic or question, the leaders of the groups need to share the group's thoughts and conclusions. They can write on the discussion sheets as well.[79]

7. The questions or sub-topics for each desk can be:
    - Why should we not modify nature for human interest?
    - Why should we make changes to nature to make human progress possible?
    - What kind of results do we have when we modify nature? Examples?
    - Will the history of human evolution look different if it did not alter our environment? How?
    - What are your concluding thoughts on 'The importance of not modifying nature'?

Round robin can be used by teachers as a strategy for brainstorming as well. It can be used to help students produce creative ideas. It is an interesting instructional tool that promotes student involvement and critical thinking. Brainstorming as a teaching tactic is used by many teachers to promote group learning. Usually, in brainstorming sessions, the teacher invites students to speak after raising their hands to contribute their knowledge and ideas. Unfortunately, not many children get the opportunity to express themselves in such settings. With the use of the round-robin discussion teaching tactic, however, each student in the group has an equal opportunity to share as everyone is asked to speak one by one.

The following are a few features of round robin that differentiate it from other brainstorming activities:

- **Equal student participation:** The most beneficial aspect of the round-robin approach is that it allows each student in the group to engage equally in the ongoing conversation. After one student starts the discussion, each student takes a turn expressing their thoughts on the topic. A teacher may use 'talking chips' or 'talking tokens' to encourage students to speak during their turn as it would require students to turn in one chip each time they express an opinion. This helps in achieving the goal of equal student participation.
- **Group discussions:** Desks are set up around the classroom in such a way that numerous brainstorming sessions can take place at the same time. Multiple teachers could be needed to oversee such discussions and to ensure that each student gets a proper chance to speak. When the brainstorming timer goes off, each group transfers to a different desk with a different topic. The round-robin discussion strategy is finished once all the groups have rotated to all the desks and discussed various topics. This allows students to debate a variety of subjects or issues while still achieving the purpose of brainstorming group discussion and that too in a limited time.[80]

Thus, activities like the one we discussed can be a useful tool to impart the skill of flexibility, which is crucial to a student's long-term success in a career. Knowing when to change, how to change and how to react *to* change are skills that pay dividends for someone's entire life.[81]

Leadership

The leadership and health educator, Ann Downer, stated that the theories associated with the terms leadership and management have evolved greatly over time. The initial concept of leadership, known as the Great Man Theory, asserted that leaders were born to lead and only the elite, wealthy aristocrats and mostly men were suitable to be leaders. This placed these groups of people on a high pedestal and thus greatly impacted representation and diversity – or the lack of it – within the workforce. Subsequently, the Great Man Theory evolved into what Downer termed the Trait Theory in which people believed that only those who inherently possessed certain traits, such as eloquence or confidence, could become effective leaders. At first glance, this might appear to be simple, direct. But when we consider the fact that those most likely to possess inherent leadership traits are the privileged, educated upper class, and still perceived to be mostly men, this leadership construct carries serious limitations according to experts.

Things, however, began to take a different turn from the 1940s, when, according to Downer, studies were undertaken, which finally begun to unpack the idea that leadership is essentially rooted in core *behaviours,* not inherent traits, natural prowess, gender or the opportunities one was afforded with when they grew up. So then, the question is: What are some of the behaviours that make a good leader in the 21st century?

1. **Emotional Intelligence and Empathy**

   Leaders today must have the ability to understand and connect with diverse individuals within their teams. They need to be fully self-aware and demonstrate a commitment to accountability and personal growth. A key element of emotional intelligence is active listening. Active listening ensures that the varied perspectives of team members are appreciated and valued. This way, leaders seek to understand where the team members are coming from and how the leader's actions will affect them, instead of going on and on with one agenda – the leader's agenda.

2. **Adaptability and Resilience**

   With the present uncertainty, change and ambiguity, in part due to economic pressures and streamlining efforts resulting in layoffs because of factors such as artificial intelligence (AI), the role of a leader becomes very significant. To be an effective leader, one needs to cultivate resilience and invest in one's professional development. Leaders need to keep abreast of trends and plan ahead in tandem with research and analysis. This way, the leader and the organization can stay flexible and respond quickly.

3. **Collaboration and Inclusivity**

   A key element of leadership in the present age is that of fostering inclusive environments to encourage diverse voices and ideas. According to a study, the greatest percentage of the workforce within a few years will be Gen Z and Millennials. And adhering to different sets of priorities of the workforce will be a crucial task for an effective leader. With a changing demography of the workforce, there can be shifts in the aspirations of team members who can no longer pursue roles with employers merely for money or the latest technology.

4. **Visionary Thinking**

   An effective leader will need to be able to craft a compelling vision. Together with the team, leaders can set a long-term objective and inspire and motivate the team to collaborate on achieving shared goals.

5. **Ethics and Responsibility**

   Of utmost importance for leaders is to prioritize ethics, integrity and sustainability in decision-making and practices. Not just talking about it; what matters is living it. Leaders must exemplify what it means to lead with transparency and integrity and to have moral leadership. To consider the impact of one's actions on others and on the environment is a green flag for leaders and team members alike.[82]

All five of these key behaviours define leadership for the present age. Experts say that traditional leadership models are inadequate. It is time for a radical transformation. The good news is that all these behaviours can be cultivated, developed and learned, even if none of them come naturally to one.[83] And this is exactly what is being discussed in this book. The reader is requested to go back to the listed qualities of an effective leader in the 21st century and mark out all those key terms and concepts that we have already been discussed in the book. The upcoming portions will help us elaborate further.

Activity: Research and Presentation

Duration: Depending on the number of groups

Instructions

1. Students to go through the following information sheets on leaders from around the globe. They need to mark out the portions where they felt the leader has displayed emotional intelligence, empathy, adaptability, resilience, collaboration, inclusivity, visionary thinking, ethics and responsibility.
2. Students can simply bracket the portion where they felt these attributes can be applied and write down the specific attribute. More than one attribute can be assigned to one leader.
3. Teachers can give students printouts of the above-mentioned attributes as references. The document can also be displayed on the class screen.

4. This part of the activity needs to be done individually by students. The following are examples of information sheets for students to study and mark.
    - Captain Lakshmi Sahgal
    - Rosa Parks
    - Martin Luther King Jr
    - Mahatma Gandhi
    - Subhas Chandra Bose

Captain Lakshmi Sahgal

Born in 1914, Lakshmi Swaminathan, commonly referred to in India as Captain Lakshmi Sehgal, was a revolutionary who took part in the Indian Independence movement, served as an officer of the Indian National Army and also worked as the minister of Women's Affairs in the Azad Hind government.

She studied medicine and received her MBBS degree from Madras Medical College in 1938. She worked as a doctor in the Government Kasturba Gandhi Hospital in Triplicane, Chennai.

In 1940, she left for Singapore, where she met some members of Subhas Chandra Bose's Indian National Army (the Azad Hind Fauj). In 1942, during the surrender of Singapore by the British to the Japanese, Lakshmi treated wounded prisoners of war, many of whom were interested in forming an Indian independence army and working towards

Indian independence. Singapore at that time had several prominent nationalist Indians working there including K.P. Kesava Menon, S.C. Guha and N. Raghavan among others. It was against this backdrop that Subhash Chandra Bose (Netaji) arrived in Singapore in July 1943 and reorganized the movement. Lakshmi Sahgal later wrote: 'At the second mass meeting, Netaji dropped a bombshell by saying that it was his intention to form a women's infantry regiment, named after the Rani of Jhansi who had fought so heroically against the British in 1857… I told him I was ready to join... The date was July 8, 1943.' Thus started the heroic journey of freedom fighters who came together to form the Azad Hind Fauj to liberate India from colonial rule.

Not only Lakshmi but many women responded enthusiastically to join the all-women brigade. Dr Lakshmi Swaminathan became Captain Lakshmi, a name and identity that would stay with her for life. She was also chosen as the minister in charge of women's organization in the Provisional Government of Free India, led by Subash Chandra Bose in Singapore.

The Azad Hind Fauj faced multiple odds and situations that were clearly not in their favour. Still, the brave soldiers of India fought without caring for their lives. Their sacrifice, valour and determination to earn freedom for their motherland inspire Indians even today.

In 1998, Captain Lakshmi Sahgal was awarded the Padma Vibhushan by Indian President K.R. Narayanan.[84]

Captain Lakshmi Sahgal[85]

Rosa Parks

Imagine you are on a bus, going to school. You bought a ticket and got yourself a seat on the bus. But the driver/ticket conductor asked you to get up from your seat to let another passenger (of a 'fairer' race) be seated, even when there are multiple empty seats on the bus. How would you feel? It is natural to feel targeted, even scared. Such was the situation in the USA some time back, which led to the civil rights movement in the country.

The civil rights movement was a social movement in the United States of America from 1954 to 1968, which aimed to abolish racial discrimination, give voting rights to all citizens and equal treatment to all people in the country. African Americans in the USA were not only discriminated against but were often treated cruelly.[86]

Rosa Parks is often referred to as the 'Mother of the Civil Rights Movement' in the United States. She became a symbol of protest when she made a brave choice that helped change unfair laws in America. She refused to give up her seat, which she had bought a valid ticket for, and was soon arrested for not following the race-based rules of the state. She observed, 'I felt that if I did stand up, it meant that I approved of the way I was being treated, and I did not approve.' Rosa Parks showed the world how one person's courage, heart and actions can make a big difference.

African Americans were treated unfairly because of their skin colour in other places as well. They had to go to separate schools, use separate water fountains and sit on separate benches, etc. These rules were called segregation laws.

In refusing to give up her seat, Rosa showed great perseverance. She stayed calm, strong and peaceful, even when the bus driver got angry. She held her ground, even when it was very dangerous. She simply said no, and that was very powerful. She stood up not just for herself but for everyone who had been hurt by racism.

Rosa believed in collaboration. Her brave act led to the Montgomery bus boycott, where African Americans stopped riding the buses for over a year. This peaceful protest helped end the unfair law. She worked with leaders like Dr Martin Luther King Jr to make further change possible. Rosa Parks believed in inclusivity. She wanted everyone to be treated equally and with kindness. She dreamed of a world where all people could live and work together in peace.

In 1963, Parks travelled to Washington, D.C. to take part in the March on Washington. Over 2,50,000 people participated in the march, and Rosa Parks was honoured alongside other prominent women in the civil rights struggle during the event's 'Tribute to Women' segment. She was arrested repeatedly, but she kept working for justice in new ways. She gave speeches, helped young people, and joined groups that fought for equal rights.

She showed resilience and advocated for civil rights although her health started worsening. Even after being arrested and threatened, Rosa kept going. She believed in standing up for what was right. She didn't just think about change; she helped create it. She trusted her vision for her country. Rosa lived with strong ethics and a sense of responsibility. She believed in doing the right thing, even when it was scary. She once said, 'You must never be fearful about what you are doing when it is right.'

Rosa Parks passed away in 2005, but her legacy lives on. Today, children all over the world learn about her in schools, and her story reminds us that there is hope for change even when the going gets tough.

Rosa Parks taught the world that courage, kindness and fairness can change history. In 2013, President Barack Obama observed February 4 as the '100th Anniversary of the Birth of Rosa Parks' and called 'upon all Americans to observe this day with appropriate service, community,

Rosa Parks[87]

and education programs to honour Rosa Parks's enduring legacy'.[88]

Martin Luther King Jr

Dr Martin Luther King Jr. is regarded by many as one of the most important leaders in American history. Born in 1929 in Atlanta, Georgia, USA, King became a prominent leader of the civil rights movement in 1955.

King took part and actively led the 1963 March on Washington, where he delivered his famous 'I Have a Dream' speech on the steps of the Lincoln Memorial. He helped to organize two of the three Selma to Montgomery marches during the 1965 Selma voting rights movement.

He, along with his fellow civil rights activists, worked towards vital laws in the country like the Civil Rights Act of 1964, the Voting Rights Act of 1965 and the Fair Housing Act of 1968. There were several instances when civil rights activists were treated brutally by racist organizations and authorities, who often responded violently.[89]

King worked to make sure all people were treated equally, no matter the colour of their skin. He believed in using peace and kindness to fight against unfair treatment. People remember him as a leader who used his heart and mind to bring change for all in his country. The following is a portion of his 'I Have a Dream' speech:

> I have a dream that one day on the red hills of Georgia the sons of former slaves and the sons of former slave owners will be able to sit down together at the table of brotherhood.
>
> I have a dream that one day even the state of Mississippi, a state sweltering with the heat of injustice, sweltering with the heat of oppression, will be transformed into an oasis of freedom and justice.
>
> I have a dream that my four little children will one day live in a nation where they will not be judged by the color of their skin but by the content of their character.
>
> I have a dream today...[90]

He believed in inclusivity, meaning everyone should be part of the dream. In his famous speech, 'I Have a Dream', King talked about a future where all children could live in peace, no matter their race. He said, 'I have a dream that one day, little Black boys and girls will join hands with little white boys and girls as sisters and brothers.'

King used the words love and non-violence to help people understand each other. He showed empathy towards all. King listened to the stories of people who were hurt by racism, and he tried to help them. He believed that everyone deserved kindness, respect and love. When peaceful marches were stopped or people were arrested, he found new ways to keep the fight for freedom going. He showed great resilience. Even when he was arrested and put in jail, he never gave up. He wrote letters, gave speeches and kept marching.

Dr Martin Luther King Jr[91]

King believed in collaboration. One of the biggest marches was the March on Washington in 1963, where over 2,50,000 people came together peacefully to protest against the ongoing injustice. He saw a better future and worked hard to make it happen. He believed in non-violence, even when others used hate or hurt him. He always chose peace and justice. He believed that being honest and doing the right thing was more important than being popular. On 14 October 1964, King won the Nobel Peace Prize for combating racial inequality through non-violent resistance.

Dr Martin Luther King Jr was unfortunately killed in 1968, but his message lives on. Today, people celebrate Martin Luther King Jr Day every January in the United States to remember his dream of love, peace and equality. The Martin Luther King Jr Memorial in the National Mall in Washington, D.C. was dedicated in 2011.[92]

Mahatma Gandhi

How Gandhi broke the Salt Law:

> **Gandhiji Breaks the Salt Law**
>
> After walking nearly 240 kilometres over many days, Mahatma Gandhi finally reached the quiet coastal village of Dandi. He had set out from Sabarmati Ashram with a clear goal, to challenge an unfair British law that made it illegal for Indians to collect or make their own salt.

The next morning, Gandhiji planned to step into the Arabian Sea and make salt with his own hands. This simple act would send a powerful message: Indians would no longer follow rules that hurt their own people.

At first, Gandhiji and his group walked without much attention. But as they neared Dandi, villagers began to join in. About two dozen men and several young boys, all wearing khadi and Gandhi topis, walked beside him. On the edge of the village, more people came, curious locals, many of them women, who greeted Gandhiji with flower petals and hopeful smiles.

Gandhiji rested at a small house near the shore, where he spent the day in quiet reflection. His followers read aloud from the Vedas, and he listened calmly.

That final stretch of the march had begun in Jalalpur, where Gandhiji had stopped the night before. By the time they reached Dandi, the tide was low. The sea had pulled back, leaving behind dry land covered in patches of bright, white salt. The sight inspired the volunteers who had come to help.

Though the police were nearby, they stayed quiet. Gandhiji joked with a visiting journalist, saying with a smile, "I will begin collecting salt at 6:30 tomorrow morning, if they let me."

This historic moment was more than about salt. It was about courage, hope, and standing up for what is right. Gandhiji showed the world that peaceful protest could shake an empire..

Mohandas Karamchand Gandhi, popularly known as Mahatma Gandhi, was one of the greatest leaders in the world. He helped India become free from British rule, not by fighting with weapons but by using peace and non-violence. People in India fondly call him 'Bapu', which means father, and also 'Mahatma', which means great soul.

Gandhi was born on 2 October 1869 in Porbandar, a small town in India. When he was young, he was shy and quiet, but he cared deeply about right and wrong. He stayed calm, even in tough situations. Gandhi cared about the poor, the sick and people who were treated unfairly. He wanted everyone in India – no matter their caste, religion or job – to be treated with respect and kindness.

Gandhi moved to South Africa in 1893 to represent an Indian merchant in a lawsuit and went on to live in South Africa for the next twenty-one years. Here, Gandhi used non-violent resistance in a campaign for civil rights. Later, he used the same ideas in India to fight for freedom. In 1915, aged forty-five, he returned to India and soon set about organizing peasants, farmers and urban labourers to protest against discrimination and excessive land tax.

Gandhi took up leadership of the Indian National Congress in 1921 and led nationwide campaigns to ease poverty, expand women's rights, build religious and ethnic unity, end untouchability, and above all, achieve swaraj or self-rule. Gandhi adopted the short dhoti woven with hand-spun yarn as a mark of identification with India's rural poor.

He began to undertake long fasts as a means of political protest.

Gandhi showed resilience, which means he never gave up. Even when he was jailed repeatedly, he stayed strong. He fasted for days to support peace and protest against violence. He wore simple clothes made from khadi and lived a simple life.

Mahatma Gandhi

Gandhi worked with many leaders like Jawaharlal Nehru, Sardar Patel and Sarojini Naidu. He also asked all Indians – men, women, children, Hindus, Muslims and people from every background – to join in the freedom movement. He wanted to end untouchability in India and for all people to be treated with dignity. He fought for the rights of women too.

Gandhi had great faith in ethical behaviour. He always told people to speak the truth and follow the path of ahimsa, or non-violence. He believed that being kind and honest was more powerful than hate or war. The concept of ahimsa has a long history in Indian religious thought and is considered the highest dharma (ethical value/virtue) to be observed towards all living beings (*sarvbhuta*), at all times (*sarvada*), in all respects (*sarvatha*), in action, words and thought.

India finally got independence from British rule on 15 August 1947. Tragically, Gandhi was killed on 30 January 1948, but his message of peace lives on. People all over the world still remember him and follow his teachings.

Mahatma Gandhi proved that you don't need to be strong with muscles – you need to be strong with your heart and mind. He was a leader who led with love, truth and peace.

Netaji Subhash Chandra Bose

Subhash Chandra Bose (fondly known as 'Netaji') gave the following speech to the Indian National Army at a rally of Indians in Burma, in 1944.

> Friends! Twelve months ago a new programme of 'total mobilisation' or 'maximum sacrifice' was placed before

Indians in East Asia. Today I shall give you an account of our achievements during the past year and shall place before you our demands for the coming year. But, before I do so, I want you to realise once again what a golden opportunity we have for winning freedom. The British are engaged in a worldwide struggle and in the course of this struggle they have suffered defeat after defeat on so many fronts. The enemy having been thus considerably weakened, our fight for liberty has become very much easier than it was five years ago. Such a rare and God-given opportunity comes once in a century. That is why we have sworn to fully utilise this opportunity for liberating our motherland from the British yoke.

I am so very hopeful and optimistic about the outcome of our struggle, because I do not rely merely on the efforts of three million Indians in East Asia. There is a gigantic movement going on inside India and millions of our countrymen are prepared for maximum suffering and sacrifice in order to achieve liberty…

…According to the programme of 'total mobilisation', I demanded of you men, money and materials. Regarding men, I am glad to tell you that I have obtained sufficient recruits already. Recruits have come to us from every corner of east Asia- from China, Japan, Indo-China, Philippines, Java, Borneo, Celebes, Sumatra, Malaya, Thailand and Burma…

You must continue the mobilisation of men, money and materials with greater vigour and energy, in particular, the problem of supplies and transport has to be solved satisfactorily.

We require more men and women of all categories for administration and reconstruction in liberated areas. We must be prepared for a situation in which the enemy will ruthlessly apply the scorched earth policy, before withdrawing from a particular area and will also force the civilian population to evacuate as was attempted in Burma…

…Now I demand more of you. Men, money and materials cannot by themselves bring victory or freedom. We must have the motive-power that will inspire us to brave deeds and heroic exploits.

It will be a fatal mistake for you to wish to live and see India free simply because victory is now within reach. No one here should have the desire to live to enjoy freedom. A long fight is still in front of us.

We should have but one desire today – the desire to die so that India may live – the desire to face a martyr's death, so that the path to freedom may be paved with the martyr's blood.

Friends! my comrades in the War of Liberation! Today I demand of you one thing, above all. I demand of you blood. It is blood alone that can avenge the blood that the enemy has spilt. It is blood alone that can pay the price of freedom. Give me blood and I promise you freedom.

His powerful words, courage and love for his country are noted by people all over the world.

This brave son of India wanted to fight the British to achieve independence. When peaceful protests were not working fast enough, he chose a different path. He believed that sometimes, stronger and bolder action was needed to attain freedom. He left India and went to countries like Germany and Japan to build support for India's freedom. He formed the Azad Hind Fauj (Indian National Army or INA) with the help of Indians living in other countries. He worked with people from different places to build an army that would fight the British and free India. In his army, he treated everyone equally. He also created a women's group called the Rani of Jhansi Regiment, where women could become soldiers. He believed that both men and women had the power to fight for freedom.

Subhas Chandra Bose was born on 23 January 1897 in Cuttack, in the state of Odisha. He was an excellent student and passed the Indian Civil Services (ICS) exam in England. But he gave that up because he wanted to fight for India's freedom. He cared deeply about people's feelings and believed that true leaders must listen and understand others. He wanted to see all Indians live with dignity and freedom. He cared about the poor, the farmers, the workers, and especially, the young people of India. He believed they were the future of the country.

Netaji Subhas Chandra Bose

Bose never gave up. Even when he was arrested, kept under watch or faced danger, he kept moving forward with courage. He believed that India must be free at any cost. His famous words, 'Give me blood, and I will give you freedom', showed how serious and passionate he was. He dreamed of a strong, independent India where all people were free and equal.

Subhas Chandra Bose was proclaimed to have died in 1945 in a plane crash, though some people believe he survived and returned to his beloved motherland. Even after his death, he is remembered as a hero who continues to inspire millions even today.

Netaji Subhas Chandra Bose showed that a true leader is brave, kind and never gives up. His life teaches us to love our country and stand up for what is right.

By practising leadership and responsibility skills, students should be able to:

1. Use interpersonal and problem-solving skills to guide and lead others. They will be able to influence, inspire and guide others towards a goal.
2. Identify and leverage the strengths of others to accomplish a common goal.
3. Be a source of inspiration for others to reach their very best. Be an example and lead selflessly.
4. Demonstrate integrity and ethical behaviour while using influence and power.
5. Be aware to act with responsibility, keeping in mind the interests of the larger community.

There are quite a large number of student leadership programmes offered at different levels – local, national and international. One such example is the MUN (Model United Nations) programme, where students simulate a United Nations meeting to deal with a specific international crisis. Here, each student delegate represents the views of a particular country. An increasing number of schools are taking part in intra- and inter-school MUNs. For young learners of grade 3 (and perhaps grade 4), the concept might be too demanding. However, a simplified version can be introduced in grade 5, given the fact that middle school MUNs are also getting popular.

Model United Nations, also known as Model UN or MUN, is an educational model of the United Nations used for simulations in which students learn about diplomacy, international relations and also get a general understanding of the UN. At a MUN conference, each learner works as the representative of a country, organization or person and must solve a problem with other delegates from around the globe.

Participation in MUNs helps students in learning skills like research, public speaking, debating, writing, critical thinking, teamwork and leadership. It is meant to engage students by allowing them to develop a deeper understanding of current world issues and world politics.[93] While MUN is typically conducted as an extracurricular activity, some schools also offer it as a class.

The Following is an example:

Students Having an Online Conference

Activity

Approximate duration: Multiple sessions can be conducted as intra-school or inter-school.

Instructions and variations:

1. Students to be divided into teams representing various UN organizations or committees, with fixed agendas.
2. Delegates (students) to come up with their opinions on a given theme and take part in a debate or discussion, where opinions can be challenged or agreed on by other delegates.
3. Delegates could also work together to suggest amendments to a UN declaration.
4. Delegates will be assigned to 'countries' and marks to be given by the Executive Body (comprised of senior students or teachers).
5. Based on the scores, delegates could be given – Best Delegate or Outstanding Delegate certificates, special mentions and verbal mentions.

Expected Outcome

Hands-on activity to better understand the procedures of the UN.

Some examples of judging criteria and points to keep in mind for MUN-ers:

1. **Speech Quality**
    - Is the delegate able to speak without reading off notes?
    - Is the delivery compelling to the other delegates?
    - Is the delegate using speech tactics like using hook, point and action?

2. **Country Accuracy**
    - Is this statement historically accurate?
    - Is this a policy that my country would actually support?

3. **Depth and Breadth of Knowledge on the Committee Topic**
    - Are the speeches and clauses nuanced, demonstrating a command of the committee topic?
    - Did the delegates talk and write about a variety of solutions that address different aspects of the committee topic?
    - Are the speeches and proposed solutions detailed, showing that the delegates have done thorough research?

4. **Branding Solutions**
    - Has the delegate attributed names and/or acronyms to the clauses and solutions so that the dais knows which solutions are from the specific delegate?

- Are the solutions proposed in the speeches actually the ones that the delegates wrote into the Working Paper and Draft Resolution?
- Is there consistency in the policy stance between their speeches and clauses?
- Did the delegate prove that the solutions are relevant to the topic at hand and integral to the bloc's Working Paper/Draft Resolution?

5. **Presentation and Q&A**
   - Is the delegate on the author's panel for the bloc's Working Paper and/or Draft Resolution?

6. **Substantially Contribute to Committee Documents**
   - How much did the delegate contribute to the bloc's Working Paper and Draft Resolution?
   - Are the solutions detailed?
   - Are there subclauses that describe the methods of implementation for the solution?
   - Did the delegate write solutions on more than one sub-topic?

7. **Bloc Leadership**
   - Has the delegate distinguished herself/himself as a leader in the bloc?
   - How helpful and inclusive was the delegate to members of the bloc?

8. **Sportsmanship/Collaboration**
   - Is the delegate kind and respectful to everyone?
   - Did the delegate do her/his absolute best to include everyone in group conversations?

9. **Research**
   - Has the delegate thoroughly researched the country and the committee topic?[94]

The NEP 2020 encourages experiential learning at all stages. Experiential learning, including hands-on learning, arts-integrated and sports-integrated education and storytelling-based pedagogy, among others, needs to be a part of standard pedagogy within each subject, with explorations of relations among different subjects. To close the gap in the achievement of learning outcomes, classroom transactions need to shift towards competency-based learning and education.[95]

It is increasingly becoming crucial for leaders to create an inclusive, collaborative work environment. Whether someone is a seasoned entrepreneur or a fresh recruit, leadership applies to their career. Setting goals and achieving those goals collaboratively are important skills not just in terms of career but also for personal growth.[96]

Initiative

Initiative can be defined as the ability to be resourceful and work without always being told what to do. Initiative requires resilience and determination. People who show initiative demonstrate skills of thinking for themselves and taking action when necessary. It means to think effectively and have the drive to achieve.

Using our initiative makes us a desirable candidate for jobs and opportunities as we indicate that we can think for ourselves, as well as prove that we will continue to develop and grow in our role. Initiative will allow us to get ahead of the competition and ensure we are up to date with what needs to be achieved. People who show good initiative often win awards and promotions as they generate exciting and beneficial ideas.[97]

It is indeed true that success requires initiative, needing students to be self-starters. Like other skills, the skill of initiative can also be learnt and practised. The rewards for students with extreme initiative vary from person to person. Sometimes, they are in the form of good grades. Other times, it can take the shape of new business ventures. Regardless, it is agreed that initiative is an attribute that earns rewards. It is especially indicative of someone's effort in terms of work ethic and professional progress.[98]

Let us take a quick look at an activity based on a comic strip

Instructions

Students to study the dialogue and answer the following questions:

a) Why do you think the student was feeling overwhelmed with the project?
b) What did the teacher advise the student to do?
c) What is initiative? How can you tell that the student took initiative?

Student: I don't think I will be able to do this project. It feels very difficult.

Teacher: The best thing to do when feeling overwhelmed is to calm yourself down and start with the basic steps that you need to start the project.

Student: Thanks teacher. You are correct. All I need to do is to start. I need to have initiative and the rest will work out as I move ahead with the project.

Teacher: Thanks, teacher!

A quick note to teachers: Comic strips are easy to make using AI. Technology has thrown up difficulties, but at the same time, has opened windows for innovation and creativity.

One can turn the dialogue above into a comic strip on any AI platform with the following set of instructions:

Please generate a comic strip with the details as followed:

Panel 1: The Overwhelmed Student

Scene: A classroom with colourful posters and a whiteboard in the background.

Characters: A young girl (around ten years old) with a messy desk full of papers, books and crayons. She has a furrowed brow and wide eyes and is gripping her hair in frustration.

Dialogue (speech bubble from student):
'I do not think I will be able to do this project! It feels too difficult!'

Panel 2: The Reassuring Teacher

Scene: The same classroom, now showing the teacher – a warm, friendly-looking woman in her thirties, kneeling beside the student's desk.

Characters: The teacher has a kind expression and a gentle posture, with one hand on the desk reassuringly.

Dialogue (speech bubble from teacher):
'The best thing to do when feeling overwhelmed is to calm

yourself down and start with the basic steps that you need to start the project.'

Panel 3: Deep Breaths

Scene: The student is sitting up straighter at her desk, eyes closed, with her hands on her chest.

Action: She's taking deep breaths – tiny animated 'breath lines' show gentle inhaling and exhaling.

Background: Slightly faded to emphasize her moment of calm and inner focus.

Panel 4: A Spark of Confidence

Scene: She opens her eyes, smiling slightly, with a light bulb icon above her head (cartoon-style).

Dialogue (Speech Bubble from the Student):
'Teacher is correct. All I need is to start! I need to have initiative, and the rest will work out as I move ahead with the project.'

Panel 5: The Thankful Hug

Scene: The student gives the teacher a big hug, her arms around the teacher's waist. Both are smiling warmly.

Characters: The teacher has one hand on the student's back, clearly touched by the moment.

Dialogue (Speech Bubble from the Student):
'Thanks, teacher!'

Here is an example of initiative taken by students to plant more trees (Geography, topic: reforestation, fighting climate change, etc.)

When children plant trees, they can learn:

- The skill of hands-on experience of changing the world. They are doing this by learning how to plant and care for a tree.
- Improving connectivity with nature and learning the skill of cooperation.
- Compassion for the environment, tree conservation.[99]
- Practising initiative and collaboration.
- Engagement with content knowledge.

An example of an organization working for planting trees by children is the Tree for Every Child Project, created by ChariTree founder and children's environmental education advocate, Andrea Koehle Jones, in cooperation with the Canadian Camping Association. The organization aims to create a fun opportunity to get children and teens outdoors while teaching them to plant trees and care about the greater community.[100]

In 2024, the *Telegraph Online* published an article on the green initiatives of residents of New Town (Kolkata). In this article, titled 'Plantation drives by New Town residents' by Snehal Gupta, the city came to know the work of a group of New Town residents comprising people from different walks of life who have successfully planted more than 2,000 saplings across the township. Apart from sourcing plants and saplings from the homes of members, the group also sources them from the forest department's Tall Tree Nursery in New Town, as well as from different nurseries in the Rajarhat area.[101]

Activity: Plantation Drive

Method/Activity: Plantation drive (interpersonal intelligence)

Topic: Global Warming (Geography)

Interpersonal intelligence can be described as the ability to discover, understand and interpret the desires and intentions of other people, thus allowing for effective social interactions. This intelligence can lead to greater adaptation to the environment, as well as the development of satisfactory social relationships. Since interpersonal intelligence promotes understanding and communication with others, taking into account their emotions, mood, motivations and intentions, possession of this ability can often be crucial in human societies.

Some of the basic characteristics of interpersonal intelligence are the following:

- People with interpersonal intelligence are seen to be interested in understanding human reasons and motivations that exist behind different behaviours and reactions. They have a high capacity for analysis and critical thinking.
- Another characteristic of people with interpersonal intelligence is good intuition in social spheres through the means of observation of and reflection on social relationships.
- Communication is very important in interpersonal intelligence, which is why people tend to be good communicators with good control of speech and non-verbal language, giving them the ability to manage and influence another person effectively.
- People with interpersonal intelligence are often able to mediate in times of conflict. Interpersonal intelligence allows a person to understand in the most objective way possible the different points of view, motivations and needs of others, which is why people usually play the role of mediator satisfactorily.
- Such people are also able to maintain old relationships since they take great care of relationships and details and are sensitive to different needs.
- These people also have excellent listening ability. They like to talk with other people, considering their points of

view and trying to understand them. This active listening helps them to get to know people and encourages acting coherently with them in the future.

- They enjoy collaborative and social projects since they are interested in human and social aspects, as well as the intercultural and individual differences of people. People with interpersonal intelligence are at ease relating to people of different ages, being able to adjust their behaviour when interacting with them.
- They also have the ability to establish new social relationships, given their orientation towards people and ease of developing healthy and satisfying social ties.[102]

What is a plantation drive?

A plantation drive is a campaign or initiative to promote the planting of trees, usually in a particular area. Be it increasing the tree cover in an area, improving the environment or ecology of the area or providing economic benefits such as employment, the goals of a plantation drive may be varied. Planting trees can help to improve the quality of air and water in a region, as well as reduce storm water run-off and provide habitat for other units of the ecosystem.[103]

Tree planting has become a cornerstone of many environmental campaigns in recent years. The call to plant trees is seen as a simple and effective way to help reduce the impact of carbon emissions and restore natural ecosystems, thus helping in combating the ill effects of global warming. Perhaps the most prominent example is the one trillion trees campaign launched by the World Economic Forum in Davos in January 2020 in support of the UN's Decade of Ecosystem Restoration. The UN declaration aims to restore, protect or plant one trillion trees by 2030. There are similar campaigns that aim to plant one trillion trees by 2050, like the one started in 2018 by nature nonprofit organizations, including the World Wildlife Fund (WWF).[104]

Such drives need the cooperation of large groups of people, often going beyond one particular organization, for instance, a school. These campaigns, then, will need interpersonal intelligence from not just students but also teachers who wish to work in a certain neighbourhood. Getting support from parents and the neighbourhood and working closely with the authorities will enable the students to assess how well-equipped they are with interpersonal communications.

On a smaller scale, plantation drives can take the form of gifting plant saplings to all members of a school community and urging them to make the world a greener place. This emphasizes the importance of interpersonal intelligence and its significance in not just learning a topic and working for a cause but also in equipping students with the skills needed to navigate the world.

The depiction of intelligence modalities, presented to you at the very beginning of the chapter, will help in understanding and answering the above questions. The diagram below relates to the theory of multiple intelligences, which states that human intelligence is not a single general ability but comprises various distinct modalities, such as linguistic, logical-mathematical, musical and spatial intelligence. The concept was introduced in 1983 by Howard Gardner in his book *Frames of Mind: The Theory of Multiple Intelligences*.

Gardner surveyed several disciplines and cultures around the world to determine skills and abilities that were deemed to be essential to human development and culture building. He observed candidates on their abilities using eight criteria that must be substantively met by each candidate to justify their identification as an *intelligence*. For Gardner, intelligence is 'a biopsychological potential to process information that can be activated in a cultural setting to solve problems or create products that are of value in a culture'. One model, which to many educators seems to fit with this framework of multiple intelligences is Bloom's taxonomy, where each intelligence can be outlined along different levels, ranging from basic knowledge up to their highest levels of analysis/synthesis.[105]

Productivity

Many think that productivity is about getting more done in less time. However, productivity is really the ability to do what you do, better.

In other words, being productive is to increase the value of your time.

Being productive is not just about working harder or faster. It is also about working smarter and assessing yourself honestly.[106]

It is an important Twenty-first century skill. It requires students to complete work effectively in an appropriate amount of time. It can also be called 'efficiency'. By understanding productivity strategies at every level, students discover the ways in which they work best while gaining an appreciation for how *others* work as well. This equips them with the practical means to carry out their goals with flexibility, leadership and initiative.[107]

The Pomodoro Technique

Pomodoro is a renowned time management technique that improves focus and productivity, regardless of the age and profession of the person using the technique.[108] It was developed in the late 1980s by Francesco Cirillo. At that time, Cirillo was a university student and was struggling to focus on his studies and assignment completion. In search of ways to combat this problem, Cirillo found a tomato-shaped kitchen timer, and thus, the idea of the Pomodoro technique was born.

The Pomodoro Technique, in essence, is a time management method that helps a person work on small chunks of a large project for 25 minutes uninterruptedly. The process involves 25 minutes of focused work and a five-minute break. This total of 30 minutes will be one Pomodoro. After four focused work sessions, a long interval of 15–20 minutes follows.[109]

How the Pomodoro Technique works:

The 25-minute focused work session and five-minute break is known to do wonders for the human brain and its performance. Here are a few things that happen when we practise the technique in our work and study.

1. Frequent short breaks help our brain to fight cognitive boredom and mental fatigue. Our focus tends to drop after 25 minutes. Therefore, it is important to have intervals to get the optimum result of our effort instead of studying for longer tenures.
2. Short breaks recharge our mind. Giving our brain time to gather new information and rest for the next challenge helps. We will start to work with a new and different perspective.

3. Focused sessions help in preventing multitasking (and the resultant mental fatigue) and procrastination. We will be more productive when we give our full attention to a single task.
4. The method motivates us to focus on the task at hand and fights Parkinson's Law.[110] (The main premise of Parkinson's Law is that the complexity of a task tends to grow the more time is allotted for its completion.)[111]
5. A five-minute break works as a reward that motivates us to work with full concentration for the scheduled 25 minutes.[112]

Since the inception of the technique, Cirillo has been working to improve the strategy to help people get more done in less time. He has written a book providing an explanation of the method and suggestions for better concentration and productivity: *The Pomodoro Technique: The Acclaimed Time-Management System that Has Transformed How We Work.*

(Pomodoro is an Italian term for tomato. Since Cirillo is from Italy and found a tomato-shaped kitchen timer, he named the method as Pomodoro Technique.)

> This technique aims to increase productivity by improving students' focus, helping them to make better choices for effective time management by staying productive during long study sessions. It also helps students with attention

deficit hyperactivity disorder (ADHD) by assisting in managing focus and providing structured breaks.[113]

The flowtime technique is a modified version of the Pomodoro Technique. It involves selecting a task and working on it until we feel we need a break. The main point here is taking breaks when needed instead of being forced to do so.

Zoe Read-Bivens introduced the Flowtime Technique in 2016 to come up with an undisrupted flow state. She customized the Pomodoro Technique by encouraging flow and introducing flexible break time and named it the Flowtime Technique.

To use the Flowtime Technique, a log/timesheet with the following specifications will be needed (on a piece of paper or digitally).

- Task name

Flowtime Log

Name: **Month:**

Date	Task Name	Start Time	Stop Time	Interruption(s)	Time Worked	Break Time
10/11/2022	Write Proposal	10:00 am	11:30 am	1	1 hour 30 mins	15 mins

A sample timesheet for the flowtime technique[115]

Activity: Using the Pomodoro Technique/Flowtime Log

Instructions

1. Students can be asked to maintain a Flowtime log or record their experience of the Pomodoro Technique while studying lengthy portions of history, geography and civics chapters.
2. It will be especially useful when students revise for term exams, where the content is lengthy.
3. Teachers can ask students to share their thoughts on the techniques in class.

Students are encouraged to set and meet goals, even in the face of obstacles and competition. This productivity skill requires students to prioritize, plan and manage work to achieve the intended results.[116]

Social Skills

The skills to become socially adept, cross-culturally fluent global learners are more important than ever before. In order to interact effectively with others, students need to:

Know when it is appropriate to listen and when it is to speak.

Conduct themselves in a respectable and professional manner.

Diverse work teams, schools and communities that are scattered around the globe but connected by technology are becoming the norm in the 21st century. In order to work effectively in diverse teams, students must respect the cultural differences between people, who may come from a wide range of social and cultural backgrounds. It is also crucial to respond with open-mindedness to different ideas and values. Social and cultural differences can be leveraged to create new ideas, innovate and improve the quality of work.[117]

The rise of social media and instant communications has changed the nature of human interaction and modes of networking. As a result, students of the 21st century might already possess a wide range of social skills. Some could be more socially adept than others. For some, socializing might come naturally.

But whether social skills come naturally to a person or not, like all skills, this needs practice too. Etiquette, manners and politeness play major roles in today's world. Giving students opportunities to learn them in an educational setting (as well as a social setting) will make them better prepared. Social skills add value to one's life.[118]

> Diversity is one thing we all have in common.
>
> – Anonymous[119]

According to research by the universities of Oxford and Reading, based on a Historical Association survey of history teachers, it was observed that some 87 per cent of the United Kingdom's secondary schools reported that they made substantial changes to history teaching to address issues of diversity. According to this report, published in 2021, the most significant reasons cited for making changes to the curriculum were a sense of social justice, to better represent the nature of history and the stimulus of recent events. Learning about 'forms of resistance or rebellion by enslaved peoples' is given equal prominence to lessons about the development of the slave trade or the campaigns in England for its abolition in schools in the UK. However, the restrictions of the curriculum of board batches might (or might not) have an effect on the diversification of the curriculum at other stages of history education in schools.[120]

For young learners studying, for example, early civilizations, it is a good idea to give them a wide range of historical experience. Learning about the Indus Valley Civilization, as well as Mesopotamian, Chinese and Egyptian civilizations, etc., can help students understand the diverse nature of the world and inculcate the skill of being aware of diversity and acknowledging the same.

The following needs to be answered by teachers to have a better understanding of themes dealing with diversity and how we can modify them according to the needs of the century.

Instructions

1. Teachers to take a look at the sample response and come up with topics from history that can be taught under the given theme.
2. The chronology of events needs to be maintained; however, teachers need to look for diverse examples.
   Sample response to the theme: Revolutions (Political)
   American Revolution (1775–1783), French Revolution (1789), Russian Revolution (February 1917) and Bolshevik Revolution (October 1917), Chinese Revolution (1945–1949), Cuban Revolution (1953–1959), etc.
   - What could the topics be for social and cultural revolution and economic and technological revolution?
   - What can the topics be for innovations in history? (Hint: fire control, agriculture, use of the wheel, paper, compass, printing press, gunpowder, steam engine, telephone, nuclear power, etc.)
   - Which topics can be categorized under the heading 'Rebellions in Asia'?

The main aim here is to understand historical facts and events from a diverse perspective to help students get the bigger picture. Make them aware not just about their past but the wider world.

A similar approach towards diversification can be achieved

in other social studies subjects. This will help learners to equip themselves with the knowledge and understanding required to hold meaningful conversations and practise their social skills.

Schools often host events throughout the year that celebrate different holidays, festivals or significant dates found in multiple cultures. These can be a great way to expose students to the concepts they are learning in the classroom and will give them first-hand knowledge of what they are studying. Another way to introduce students to diverse people and cultures is by bringing people of diverse backgrounds into the classroom. This can be an opportunity to bring parents into class or experts from perhaps a local college/university, a multicultural organization, etc.

A quick way to display diverse cultures in the classroom is to include bulletin boards and instructions in a number of languages. Teachers can use tools like Google Translate to come up with the right terminology.[121] Class discussions on why we are diverse and what we have in common can lead to sharing by students and teachers.

Activity: Fill in the word bubbles!

Duration: 15 minutes

Instructions

1. Students to name each of the children on the worksheet below.

2. Next, they will need to use the picture clues and their own imagination to fill in the word bubbles. The children here are introducing themselves to the entire group. Students to keep in mind that the responses need to be appropriate, polite and relatable to the children shown in the pictures.

Chapter 6

Conclusion

AS THE AMERICAN PHILOSOPHER, education reformer John Dewey would say, Education is not just a preparation for life; it is indeed life in itself.

And like all other aspects of human life, education needs to have reforms, policies and ideas which guide us towards achieving our full potential. The National Education Policy 2020 is seen to be one such endeavour to develop an education system which promoted good human beings capable of rational thought and action, possessing compassion and empathy, courage and resilience, scientific temper and creative imagination. These individuals with their sound ethical approaches and values must aim to become engaged, productive and contributing citizens of the country. A country which is built on the foundations of equitability, inclusivity and plurality, as envisaged by our Constitution.[122]

Whether we take the help of the Twenty-first century skills or any other teaching–learning cornerstones, the end goal is to give our learners a chance towards holistic development. Critical thinking, information literacy, creativity are such skills which tap into the mental processes involved in learning, such as understanding, memory and problem-solving. Cognitivism focuses on the idea that students process information they receive rather than just responding to a stimulus. Cognitive theories were known to have developed in the early 1900s in Germany by Wolfgang Köhler. Cognitivism has given rise to many evidence-based education theories, including cognitive load theory, schema theory and dual coding theory. In cognitivism theory, learning occurs when the student reorganizes information, either by finding new explanations or adapting old ones. Any discussion on the cognitive learning theories is incomplete without mentioning Jean Piaget, a pioneer when it comes to studying cognitive experiences of children.[123]

Behaviorist strategies help in accumulating important skills by building productivity, accountability, and technology literacy in learners. This can be in form of structured practice, feedback, and setting up of performance benchmarks. Behaviorism is based on the idea that knowledge is independent of the learner. In a behaviorist's mind, the learner is a blank slate, who should be provided with the information to be learnt. While another prominent learning theory – Constructivism –

states that we construct learning new ideas based on our own prior knowledge and experiences. Learning, therefore, is unique to the individual learner. Learners are seen to adapt their models of understanding either by reflecting on prior theories or resolving misconceptions. (For example, the steps involved in Bruner's Spiral Curriculum.)[124] Skills like collaboration, communication, cultural awareness and creativity align learners with the idea of constructivism by considering learners as active participants in building their own knowledge through experiences and collaboration.

Thus, teaching-learning is a complex interlinked process; NEP 2020, Twenty-first century skills, learning theories, the teachers' experiences, the students' contribution and many other factors, elements come together to form our education systems.

Notes

1. https://www.education.gov.in/sites/upload_files/mhrd/files/NEP_Final_English.pdf
2. https://www.education.gov.in/sites/upload_files/mhrd/files/NEP_Final_English.pdf, 5–6.
3. https://www.education.gov.in/sites/upload_files/mhrd/files/NEP_Final_English.pdf
4. https://ncf.ncert.gov.in/webadmin/assets/ba0dd5d8-b8f9-4315-9e14-403752acdc26, 23–24.
5. https://ncf.ncert.gov.in/webadmin/assets/ba0dd5d8-b8f9-4315-9e14-403752acdc26, 320.
6. https://pressbooks.pub/techandcurr2019/chapter/pbl-competencies/
7. Bernie Trilling, Charles Fadel, *21st Century Skills, Learning for Life in Our Times*, 111.
8. https://www.linkedin.com/pulse/conducting-effective-focus-group-discussions-guide-hr-gaurav-bhatli-9oujc/
9. https://themba.institute/business-communication/group-discussion/
10. https://journals.sagepub.com/doi/full/10.3102/0034654320933544
11. https://en.wikipedia.org/wiki/Flipped_classroom
12. https://www.tandfonline.com/doi/full/10.1080/00131881.2020.1836987#d1e231
13. https://www.scribbr.com/frequently-asked-questions/why-essays-college-applications/#:~:text=The%20college%20essay%20may%20be%20the%20deciding%20factor,such%20as%20why%20you%20chose%20that%20specific%20college.

14. https://learn.agileclassrooms.com/blog/why-Twenty-first Century-skills-matter
15. https://www.edalex.com/guides/Twenty-first Century-skills-what-they-are-why-important/
16. By Armpam: Own work, CC BY-SA 4.0, https://commons.wikimedia.org/w/index.php?curid=117919127
17. https://en.wikipedia.org/wiki/Armstrong_Pame
18. https://www.youtube.com/watch?v=gmfcihpxXig
19. https://en.wikipedia.org/wiki/Armstrong_Pame
20. By Armpam: Own work, CC BY-SA 4.0, https://commons.wikimedia.org/w/index.php?curid=117833221
21. https://www.icevonline.com/blog/what-are-Twenty-first Century-skills
22. Bernie Trilling, Charles Fadel, *21st Century Skills, Learning for Life in Our Times*, 39.
23. Bernie Trilling, Charles Fadel, *21st Century Skills, Learning for Life in Our Times*, 38.
24. Bernie Trilling, Charles Fadel, *21st Century Skills, Learning for Life in Our Times*, 38.
25. https://theindianconstitution.com/article-24-child-labour-prohibition/
26. Bernie Trilling, Charles Fadel, *21st Century Skills, Learning for Life in Our Times*, 50.
27. https://www.icevonline.com/blog/what-are-Twenty-first Century-skills
28. Ryan D. Shaw, 'How Critical Is Critical Thinking?' *Music Educators Journal*, vol. 101, no. 2, 2014, 65–70. *JSTOR:* http://www.jstor.org/stable/43288924. Accessed 15 May 2025.
29. https://www.icevonline.com/blog/what-are-Twenty-first Century-skills
30. https://en.wikipedia.org/wiki/Riddle

31. https://showora.com/the-hobbit-riddles-answers/
32. By Leonardo da Vinci: Cropped and relevelled from File. Leonardo da Vinci, *Mona Lisa*, from C2RMF.jpg. Originally C2RMF: Galerie de tableaux en très haute définition: image page, Public Domain, https://commons.wikimedia.org/w/index.php?curid=15442524
33. https://dictionary.cambridge.org/dictionary/english/cognition
34. https://en.wikipedia.org/wiki/Cognition
35. https://en.wikipedia.org/wiki/Cognitivism_(psychology)
36. https://www.growthengineering.co.uk/learning-theories/
37. Bernie Trilling, Charles Fadel, *21st Century Skills, Learning for Life in Our Times*, 57.
38. https://www.icevonline.com/blog/what-are-Twenty-first Century-skills
39. Danah Henriksen, et al., 'Infusing Creativity and Technology in 21st Century Education: A Systemic View for Change', *Journal of Educational Technology & Society*, vol. 19, no. 3, 2016, pp. 27–37. *JSTOR:* http://www.jstor.org/stable/jeductechsoci.19.3.27. Accessed 15 May 2025.
40. https://www.education.gov.in/sites/upload_files/mhrd/files/NEP_Final_English.pdf
41. https://www.ourendangeredworld.com/india/
42. https://www.futurelearn.com/info/courses/creativity-neuroscience/0/steps/258336
43. https://www.inc.com/annabel-acton/10-einstein-quotes-to-fire-up-your-creativity.html
44. https://www.icevonline.com/blog/what-are-Twenty-first Century-skills
45. https://www.classpoint.io/blog/team-building-activities-for-collaboration
46. https://theecmconsultant.com/what-is-collaboration/

47. https://www.azquotes.com/quotes/topics/effective-communication.html
48. https://www.icevonline.com/blog/what-are-Twenty-first Century-skills
49. https://www.collegenp.com/article/10-proven-ways-to-improve-communication-skills
50. https://www.linkedin.com/pulse/lessons-collaboration-from-vallam-kali-kerala-boat-race-training-u85bf
51. https://www.wikihow.com/Play-Simon-Says
52. https://zaided.com/active-listening-activities-for-students/
53. https://www.twinkl.co.in/blog/13-feedback-activities-for-esl-students
54. https://www.growthtactics.net/empathy-building-activities/
55. Bernie Trilling, Charles Fadel, *21st Century Skills, Learning for Life in Our Times*, 49.
56. https://www.icevonline.com/blog/what-are-Twenty-first Century-skills
57. Sally Valentino Drew, 'Open Up the Ceiling on the Common Core State Standards: PREPARING STUDENTS FOR Twenty-first Century LITERACY—NOW', *Journal of Adolescent & Adult Literacy*, vol. 56, no. 4, 2012, 321–30. *JSTOR:* http://www.jstor.org/stable/23367702. Accessed 16 May 2025.
58. Stephan De Spiegeleire, et al, 'AI – TODAY AND TOMORROW', *ARTIFICIAL INTELLIGENCE AND THE FUTURE OF DEFENSE: STRATEGIC IMPLICATIONS FOR SMALL- AND MEDIUM-SIZED FORCE PROVIDERS*, Hague Centre for Strategic Studies, 2017, 43–59. *JSTOR:* http://www.jstor.org/stable/resrep12564.8. Accessed 16 May 2025.
59. https://www.icevonline.com/blog/what-are-Twenty-first Century-skills

60. https://ncert.gov.in/textbook/pdf/kefa101.pdf
61. By Raveesh Vyas: originally posted to Flickr as Bhimbetka Cave Paintings, CC BY-SA 2.0, https://commons.wikimedia.org/w/index.php?curid=7756171
62. https://mausam.imd.gov.in/Forecast/marquee_data/Press%20 Release%2016-05-2025.pdf
63. All correct sentences: *Oxford Primary Social Studies*, (Oxford University Press, 2015)
64. Bernie Trilling, Charles Fadel, *21st Century Skills, Learning for Life in Our Times*, 69–70.
65. https://en.wikipedia.org/wiki/Technological_literacy
66. https://www.icevonline.com/blog/what-are-Twenty-first Century-skills
67. https://en.wikipedia.org/wiki/Technological_literacy
68. https://parade.com/937586/parade/life-quotes/
69. https://en.wikipedia.org/wiki/Life_skills
70. https://www.iosrjournals.org/iosr-jhss/papers/Vol.27-Issue4/Ser-9/H2704096065.pdf
71. https://www.iosrjournals.org/iosr-jhss/papers/Vol.27-Issue4/Ser-9/H2704096065.pdf
72. https://www.icevonline.com/blog/what-are-Twenty-first Century-skills
73. https://en.wikipedia.org/wiki/Life_skills
74. Bernie Trilling, Charles Fadel, *21st Century Skills, Learning for Life in Our Times*, 75.
75. https://www.icevonline.com/blog/what-are-Twenty-first Century-skills
76. Bernie Trilling, Charles Fadel, *21st Century Skills, Learning for Life in Our Times*, 77.
77. https://k12.thoughtfullearning.com/FAQ/what-are-life-skills#:~:text=The%2021st%20century%20life%20skills%20

are%20flexibility%2C%20initiative%2C,to%20adjust%20 and%20adapt%20is%20critical%20to%20success.

78. https://www.bigrentz.com/blog/earthquake-proof-buildings
79. https://blog.teachmint.com/ultimate-guide-to-the-round-robin-approach/
80. https://blog.teachmint.com/ultimate-guide-to-the-round-robin-approach/
81. https://www.icevonline.com/blog/what-are-Twenty-first Century-skills
82. https://www.forbes.com/sites/rachelwells/2024/03/12/what-is-leadership-a-new-definition-for-2024/
83. https://www.forbes.com/sites/rachelwells/2024/03/12/what-is-leadership-a-new-definition-for-2024/
84. https://en.wikipedia.org/wiki/Lakshmi_Sahgal
85. https://www.thestatesman.com/wp-content/uploads/2022/08/Brown-Minimalist-Furniture-Photo-Collage-1-1024x683.jpg
86. https://en.wikipedia.org/wiki/Civil_rights_movement
87. *Ebony* Magazine, Original publication, Originally on Wikimedia Commons, NARA copy here (ID 470863696), Fair use, https://en.wikipedia.org/w/index.php?curid=79877646
88. https://en.wikipedia.org/wiki/Rosa_Parks
89. https://en.wikipedia.org/wiki/Martin_Luther_King_Jr
90. https://www.history.com/articles/i-have-a-dream-speech
91. By Nobel Foundation: Description page (direct link), Public Domain, https://commons.wikimedia.org/w/index.php?curid=9719576
92. https://en.wikipedia.org/wiki/Martin_Luther_King_Jr
93. https://en.wikipedia.org/wiki/Model_United_Nations#:~:text=Model%20United%20Nations%2C%20also%20known%20as%20Model%20UN,which%20students%20learn%20about%20diplomacy%20and%20international%20relations

94. https://www.harvardmun.org/resources-for-preparation
95. https://www.education.gov.in/sites/upload_files/mhrd/files/NEP_Final_English.pdf, 12.
96. https://www.icevonline.com/blog/what-are-Twenty-first Century-skills
97. https://www.youthemployment.org.uk/what-is-initiative-and-why-is-it-important/#:~:text=Initiative%20is%20the%20ability%20to%20be%20resourceful%20and,your%20head%2C%20and%20having%20the%20drive%20to%20achieve
98. https://www.icevonline.com/blog/what-are-Twenty-first Century-skills
99. https://www.charitree-foundation.org/a-tree-for-every-child/
100. https://www.charitree-foundation.org/a-tree-for-every-child/
101. https://www.telegraphindia.com/west-bengal/kolkata/plantation-drives-by-new-town-residents/cid/2034411
102. https://psychologyfor.com/interpersonal-intelligence-what-it-is-examples-and-activities-to-improve-it/
103. https://aftonvilla.com/the-benefits-of-a-plantation-drive/
104. https://www.globalcitizen.org/en/content/why-planting-trees-helps-fight-climate-change/
105. https://en.wikipedia.org/wiki/Theory_of_multiple_intelligences
106. https://ilampadman.com/top-productivity-skills-for-the-busy-professional
107. https://www.icevonline.com/blog/what-are-Twenty-first Century-skills
108. https://timehackz.com/time-management-activities-for-students/
109. https://timehackz.com/is-the-pomodoro-technique-effective-for-studying/

110. https://timehackz.com/is-the-pomodoro-technique-effective-for-studying/
111. https://www.verywellmind.com/what-is-parkinsons-law-6674423
112. https://timehackz.com/is-the-pomodoro-technique-effective-for-studying/
113. https://sketchplanations.com/the-pomodoro-technique
114. https://timehackz.com/flowtime-technique/
115. https://i0.wp.com/timehackz.com/wp-content/uploads/2022/11/Flowtime-Log.jpg
116. Bernie Trilling, Charles Fadel, *21st Century Skills, Learning for Life in Our Times*, 83.
117. Bernie Trilling, Charles Fadel, *21st Century Skills, Learning for Life in Our Times*, 80–81.
118. https://www.icevonline.com/blog/what-are-Twenty-first Century-skills
119. Bernie Trilling, Charles Fadel, *21st Century Skills, Learning for Life in Our Times*, 80.
120. https://www.ox.ac.uk/news/2021-10-22-history-teaching-has-substantially-changed-address-diversity-say-teachers
121. https://pce.sandiego.edu/10-ways-to-teach-diversity-in-the-classroom/
122. https://www.education.gov.in/sites/upload_files/mhrd/files/NEP_Final_English.pdf
123. https://www.educationcorner.com/learning-theories-in-education/
124. https://www.educationcorner.com/learning-theories-in-education/

Image Copyright Information

1. **Armstrong Pame** – Armpam, CC BY-SA 4.0 <https://creativecommons.org/licenses/by-sa/4.0>, via Wikimedia Commons
2. **Construction of People's Road** – Armpam, CC BY-SA 4.0 <https://creativecommons.org/licenses/by-sa/4.0>, via Wikimedia Commons
3. **Mona Lisa** – Public Domain
4. **Bhimbhetka Cave Painting 1** – Bernard Gagnon, CC BY-SA 3.0 <https://creativecommons.org/licenses/by-sa/3.0>, via Wikimedia Commons
5. **Bhimbetka Cave Painting 2** – Raveesh Vyas, CC BY-SA 2.0 <https://creativecommons.org/licenses/by-sa/2.0>, via Wikimedia Commons
6. **Grey-headed Fish Eagle** – Charles J. Sharp, CC BY-SA 4.0 <https://creativecommons.org/licenses/by-sa/4.0>, via Wikimedia Commons
7. **Dugong** – Vkilikov/Shutterstock.com
8. **Indian Softshell Turtle** – Sourabh Bharti/Shutterstock.com
9. **Sun Temple** – Jitendra M Parmar/Shutterstock.com
10. **Captain Lakshmi Sahgal** – Soman, CC BY-SA 3.0 <http://creativecommons.org/licenses/by-sa/3.0/>, via Wikimedia Commons
11. **Rosa Parks** – Kingkongphoto & www.celebrity-photos.com from Laurel Maryland, USA, CC BY-SA 2.0 <https://creativecommons.org/licenses/by-sa/2.0>, via Wikimedia Commons
12. **Martin Luther King Jr** – Nobel Foundation, Public domain, via Wikimedia Commons

13. **Mahatma Gandhi** – Elliott & Fry, Public domain, via Wikimedia Commons
14. **Netaji Subhas Chandra Bose** –Unknown (Netaji Research Bureau, Calcutta), Public domain, via Wikimedia Commons
15. **Students having an online conference** – Media_Photos/ Shutterstock.com